The 50 in HAWAII

The Ultimate Guide
to the
Essential Sites

By TIM ROCK & DAVID FLEETHAM

Breaching humpback

About This Book

*From **Tim*** - Hawaii is an amazing US state with so many opportunities to photograph sea creatures great and small. And after the diving, the ever-evolving geography never fails to bring even more eye-popping photo ops. The late Jim Watt taught me a huge appreciation for the whales in these waters. My own travels have also led me to appreciate the other unique marine mammals and the island culture. *From **David*** - As a photographer I have been fortunate to dive all over the world and I can assure you it is never disheartening to come home. To this day, a week rarely goes by where I do not get to photograph the underwater world off my home on Maui. Each year I travel to one or more of my neighboring islands to experience what they have to offer. In this book, we hope to show you just why the Hawaiian waters are so special.

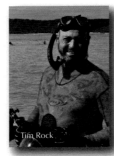
Tim Rock

About the Authors:
Tim Rock is an internationally published photojournalist who specializes in the ocean realm. Based on Guam in the Western Pacific Ocean, Rock has traveled Micronesia, the Indo-Pacific and worldwide for three decades. He has visited and dived in Hawaii many times. He is a recipient of the University of Nebraska-Omaha Dept. of Communications Lifetime Achievement Award. He is the author of numerous Lonely Planet Diving & Snorkeling guides and is represented by Getty Images Lonely Planet Collection. His website: **http://www. doubleblue. com**

David Fleetham

David Fleetham After ten years of working in various dive businesses in Vancouver, Canada, David had the opportunity for employment as a dive guide/instructor in Maui. That was 1986 and Hawaii has been his home ever since. He has done National Geographic assignments and leads tours and acts as a photographic teacher and judge in many international photo contests. He is recognized as one of the world's best underwater photographers. He uses Ikelite equipment and flies DJI drones as well. His work can be found here: **http://www. davidfleetham. com**

Photographic Equipment Used
Rock uses Aquatica and underwater housings, Panasonic mirrorless photo gear, Ikelite strobes and TLC arms. Fleetham uses Ikelite Housings and Strobes and Canon cameras. Both fly DJI drones. All photos by the authors unless otherwise noted. **Disclaimer:** The authors have taken all reasonable care in preparing this book. They make no warranty about the accuracy and completeness of its content and, to the maximum extent permitted, disclaim all liability from its use. ©2020 MantaRay Publishing, All Rights Reserved. This book may not be copied in ANY form. **Cover Photo**: Diver entering First Cathedral on Maui by David Fleetham.

An ancient Hawaiian platform or Heiau at Kamakahonu Beach, once the residence of King Kamehameha I,

How to Use This Book

The intent of this book is entertainment and practical information for what the authors consider the cream of the crop of Hawaii's many scuba diving and snorkeling sites. You will **not** find GPS coordinates or specific mooring instructions in this book. It is not intended for independent sailors or boaters. We hope, to maximize your fun and safety while diving in the state, you will use an experienced Hawaiian dive operation. It is our experience that ocean conditions can change quickly and we feel using a professional diving operation is the best way to ensure a fun, safe and informative vacation. Trip Advisor and other internet outlets list many of the current dive ops for your online convenience. This book is intended to give you insights to what we, as the authors, feel are the most interesting, unique, exciting and popular sites in this special USA state. We hope you will be able to read through this candy store of great Hawaiian dive sites and enjoy some (or all!!) of the best diving Hawaii has to offer.

Humpback breach, Kona

HAWAII'S
TOP 50
Diving & Snorkeling Sites

Spinner dolphins and snorkeler

Ukelele player, Kona

Overview

It is a vivid memory still to this day. I was working at The Diving Locker in Vancouver, Canada. Raindrops were dancing off the pavement on the street as Jim, a fellow diving instructor and old friend, dashed in dripping and said he bought a dive shop in Lahaina, Maui and moved his 48' sailboat down there. He needed someone to live on the boat and he would get me a job in the dive shop. Just then, the sun popped out and a rainbow appeared over Kitsilano. I asked if this was some sort of a trick question. I said sure and thought "I could do that for a year".

That was 1986. Six years later the shop was gone. The boat was gone. I stayed and made Maui my home. There have been many changes in my thirty-plus years, but the surrounding Pacific Ocean still has me jumping in at least once a week.

Home to the world's most active volcanoes, the only royal palace in the U. S. and the welcoming "Aloha Spirit"— Hawaii is like no place on earth. Discover the shimmering ocean, emerald valleys and golden sands; get lost in the beauty of the hula and the strum of a ukelele and find out in this book how the warmth of Hawaii's people wonderfully complement the amazing ocean here in my home state.
- *David Fleetham*

Gecko on a banana leaf

Hawaii at a Glance

A view of Science City atop Haleakela Crater Rim, the white astronomy buildings top right, from Upcountry Maui

History

The history of Hawaii describes the era of human settlements in the Hawaiian Islands. That history begins sometime between 124 and 1120 AD, when the islands were first settled by Polynesians. Hawaiian civilization was isolated from the rest of the world for at least 500 years.

Europeans, led by British explorer James Cook, arrived in the Hawaiian Islands in 1778. However, some researchers state the Spanish captain Ruy López de Villalobos was the first European to see the islands in 1542. Within five years after Cook's arrival, European military technology helped King Kamehameha I conquer and unify the islands for the first time, establishing the Kingdom of Hawaii. The kingdom was prosperous and important for its agriculture and strategic Pacific location

American immigration began almost immediately after Cook's arrival, led by Protestant missionaries. Americans set up plantations to grow sugar. Their methods of plantation farming required a lot of human labor. Waves of permanent immigrants came from

Big wave surfing at the famous JAWS surf break (Peahi)

Japan, China and the Philippines to work in the fields. The government of Japan organized and gave special protection to its people, who, by 1896, comprised about 25 percent of the Hawaiian population .

The native population succumbed to disease (particularly smallpox) brought by the Europeans, declining from 300,000 in the 1770s to over 60,000 in the 1850s to 24,000 in 1920.

Americans within the kingdom government rewrote the constitution, severely curtailing the power of King "David" Kalākaua, and disenfranchising the rights of most Native Hawaiians and Asian citizens to vote, through excessively high property and income requirements. This gave a sizeable advantage to plantation owners. Queen Liliuokalani attempted to restore royal powers in 1893, but was placed under house arrest by businessmen with help from the US military. Against the

Queen's wishes, the Republic of Hawaii was formed for a short time.

This government agreed on behalf of Hawaii to join the US in 1898 as the Territory of Hawaii. In 1959, the islands became the state of Hawaii of the United States.

Hawaii's rich past comes to vivid life at incredible historic sites that help us understand the historical, cultural and environmental forces that shaped Hawaii as we know it today. Whether it's a unique natural wonder, a National Historic Site, Park or Monument or a sacred place that connects us to Native Hawaiian customs, beliefs and practices, these sites will help you gain a deeper understanding of Hawaii.

Diving History

Marine biologists suggest that 100,000 years may have passed between species reaching the islands to

Waterfalls tumble down the hills behind Wai'oli Hui'ia Church in the town of Hanalei, Kauai, Hawaii.

develop to what we see now. This isolation made it impossible for species like clownfish and their anemones to get to Hawaii. Clownfish, once they hatch from eggs, have a larval state that lasts but a few weeks. Even with the closest and fastest passing of currents, the larvae don't have enough time to reach Hawaii. Yellow tangs, on the other hand, can last for several months in open ocean before they need to find a reef to call home. And so, yellow tangs are abundant in Hawaii.

As the dinosaurs in Jurassic Park confirmed, "life will find a way" and sure enough the fish in Hawaii did as well. Jurassic Park by the way was filmed on Kauai, but back to the fish. Some species, unable to find a mate that possessed a resemblance to themselves, chose to attempt a cross species fertilization that occasionally resulted in an entirely new species of fish. This phenomenon is rare in most

oceans, but surprisingly common in Hawaii. Over twenty-five percent of the fish in Hawaii are endemic. Some of these "only in Hawaii" fish are rarely seen and highly valued by fish collectors. Others, such as the millet seed butterflyfish or the saddleback wrasse, make up some of the most numerous fish to be seen on Hawaii's reefs.

Dive shops first popped up in 1960 in Oahu and have spread to all of the major islands. Jack Clothier, a NAUI Instructor, NAUI Course Director, and NAUI branch manager for Hawaii and the West Pacific was also one of the original owners of BoJack's Dive Center on Oahu. He was instrumental in bringing sport diving to the state of Hawaii in the 1970s. He then opened Jack's Diving Locker at Kona in 1981. One notable diver in the late 1980s, Jerry Garcia, lead guitarist and vocalist of the Grateful Dead, came to Jack's

Lava flow on Hawaii's Big Island

and was so impressed with Kona diving he testified at a Hawaii state hearing in support of a mooring buoy project.

Black coral diving is one of the most famous legacies beginning in 1958 with Jack Ackerman and ending with Captain Robin Lee passing in 2012. Collecting rare black coral for jewelry at depths well below sport diving, a handful of men worked in a dangerous industry for many decades until the practice was stopped in 2012.

Geography

Not long ago molten rock began to flow upwards from the ocean floor to form the archipelago known as the Hawaiian Islands. At least, not long ago if you are a geologist. Forty-million years later, the eight main islands that most people think of as Hawaii, actually represent the most recent volcanic peaks in the long line of a submerged mountain range which stretches to the northwest for almost 1600 miles. Millions of years of erosion have taken their toll on these great mountain tops. North, beyond Kauai, all that remains of the peaks are small atolls, reefs and shoals. As you move south, the land is geologically younger.

The Big Island, at the southern end of the state, is made up of five shield volcanos, and is still in the process of island making. Here lava has been flowing from Kilauea volcano since 1983 and still reaches the ocean in a spectacle of steam and splattering rock that must be seen to be comprehended. Underwater, the lava cools to form a crust which bursts as pressure from the flow builds. The ongoing explosions make diving unadvisable. Thirty miles southeast of Hawaii, a new island is forming. Loihi, as it has been named, is working it's way up from the sea floor, and is now 3000ft (900m) from the

An aerial view of Ko Olina beaches and resorts on the West Side of Oahu

Feral axis deer came to Maui 1867

surface. It will be another million years before it rises out of the Pacific, and I understand hotel entrepreneurs will have time-shares available soon.

Initially these islands were lifeless black volcanic monoliths. Because they were further from the continents than any other island group on the planet, geologists believe it took millions of years for life to find its way here.

Today Hawaii boasts a snow-capped peak and a deep offshore valley with so many different geographical and geological formations in between, it is unique in the world. This attracts big marine life as well in the deep water.

Grow Food

Plants for sale at Sunday fair, Big Island

Hawaiian Language & Culture

Young woman participates in traditional Hawaiian ceremony. Puu Pehe Rock is in the background.
© Hawaii Tourism Authority (HTA) / Joe West

The Hawaiian language, 'Ōlelo Hawaii, came to our shores along with the first people to arrive from the ancestral homelands of Polynesia. The language evolved alongside the culture into the nuanced, multi-layered 'Ōlelo Hawaii today.

When the written language was introduced to the masses in the early 1800s, Hawaii residents – both Native Hawaiians and others who came to the islands – developed an insatiable appetite for reading and writing in 'Ōlelo Hawaii. Newspapers with news of Hawaii and the wonders of the world made their way to all corners of the kingdom. Literacy rates rivaled the most progressive nations in the world. The cosmopolitan citizenry of the Hawaiian kingdom conducted their lives in Hawaiian, the language of the land.

Following the overthrow of the Hawaiian kingdom in 1893, Hawaiian language use declined along with other

Large carvings at the Pu'uhonua o Hōnaunau National Historical Park on the Kona Coast

Eating Hawaiian bar-b-q on the Kona Aggressor

Hawaiian cultural practices, lifestyles, and arts. Aiding in the decline was a law banning instruction in the language in Hawaii schools.

The Hawaiian cultural renaissance of the 1970s set the stage for the language's return from the brink of extinction. Sparked by the realization that fewer than 50 children spoke the language in the early 1980s, a group of educators established preschools where children learned Hawaiian by interacting with native speaking elders. These schools proved successful and today are the foundation of an educational system where students can go as far as a doctoral degree in the language.

Even with Hawaiian language returning to prominence in Hawaii, the only state in the US with two official languages, it is still classified as a critically endangered language by the United Nations.

According to GoHawaii.com, you too can be a part of the 'Ōlelo Hawaii revival. Start with the basic Hawaiian words and pronunciation tips below. When you arrive, use Hawaiian place names whenever possible. A growing number of businesses are incorporating 'Ōlelo Hawaii into their signage. When you arrive at your hotel, ask what Hawaiian language resources are available. And remember to greet the people you meet with a warm, genuine "Aloha".

Useful Hawaiian Phrases

Aloha ahiahi!	Good evening!
Aloha awakea!	Good day!
(generally 11am - 1pm)	
Aloha e _____!	Greetings _____!
Aloha 'auinalā!	Good afternoon!
Aloha kakahiaka!	Good morning!
Aloha kākou!	Greetings to all

A Hawaiian fisherman cleaning
fresh fish at the dock

Island entrepreneurs

Hawaii Practicalities

Climate

Weather in The Hawaiian Islands is very consistent, with only minor changes in temperature throughout the year. There are really only two seasons in Hawaii: summer (kau) from May to October and winter (hooilo) from November to April. The average daytime summer temperature at sea level is 85F (29.4C), while the average daytime winter temperature is 78F (25.6C). Temperatures at night are approximately 10F lower than the daytime.

The islands are an incredible collection of diverse micro-environments, each with its own unique weather plants and animals. As a result of the shielding effect of volcanic mountains and the differences in weather at various elevations, you can find tropical rainforests, cool alpine regions, arid deserts and sunny beaches—all within the span of just a few miles.

Throughout the year, Hawaiian weather patterns are affected primarily by high-pressure zones in the north Pacific that pump cool, moist trade winds down onto the islands' northeastern slopes. These winds are forced upslope by the mountain heights,

Blossoms on a jacaranda tree beside the road to Haleakala Crater on Maui.

where their moisture condenses into clouds that produce rain. Most of the rain falls in the mountains and valleys on the windward (northeastern) side of the islands. It is this weather phenomenon that creates Hawaii's rich, green, tropical environment.

The wettest months are from November to March, but winter rains do not generally disrupt dive vacation plans, since the weather is localized. This means that if it is raining where you are, there is almost always a sunny spot to be found around the coast.

The Hawaiian Islands' trade winds mean there is almost always a cooling breeze. Several times during the year the trade winds will stop completely and the wind will switch around to come out of the south or west, bringing stormy or hot, sticky weather. Islanders sometimes call this kona weather, because kona means leeward or south, and this points to the direction from

which these weather systems arrive.

The Hawaiian Islands' nearshore water temperatures remain comfortable throughout the year. The average water temperature is 74F (23.3C), with a summer high of 80F (26.7C). Wave action varies dramatically between island coasts and seasons. Summer waters are typically gentle on all beaches. During the winter on many north shore beaches, Pacific storms drive ocean swells toward the islands, creating the Hawaiian islands' legendary big waves.

Wave conditions are often very localized, so if the waves are too big on your beach, you can usually find calmer water at a more sheltered beach. Strong currents can make any beach unsafe at any time during the year, particularly in the winter. Ask your hotel staff or a lifeguard about ocean currents or look for warning flags and posted beach conditions.

The saffron finch can be spotted in many places throughout the islands.

Please heed all weather warnings before hiking, swimming, sailing or participating in any outdoor activities.

Getting There

Hawaii is served by a host of airlines internationally. The main airport is Honolulu International Airport (HNL). HNL is also Hawaii's major airport, serving as the entry point for most of Hawaii's visitors.

Getting Around

Once you're in Hawaii, it's simple to get around. If you're planning to stay in Waikiki, you can get around by shuttle, tour bus, taxi or Hawaii's excellent public transportation system. But to really experience Oahu outside of Waikiki, you should consider renting a car at Honolulu International Airport. The same goes for Hawaii's other islands, all of which have vehicle rentals. Depending on your dive schedule, (if you're joining a liveaboard you won't need a car) a car is the best way to get to your dive shop and also to local eateries and back and forth from the hotel. Some shops have pick-up service so talk with your operator before you go.

It is easy and fast to get to and explore the other Hawaiian Islands. Multiple carriers (including Hawaiian Airlines, Southwest and Mokulele Airlines) offer short flights between islands. You may need to connect through Oahu to reach neighbor islands. When traveling interisland, it is recommended that you arrive at least 90 minutes prior to your flight.

Flight times from Daniel K. Inouye

(Honolulu) International Airport (HNL), Oahu to:

Lihue Airport (LIH), Kauai: 30 minutes

Kahului Airport (OGG), Maui: 30 minutes

Kapalua-West Maui Airport (JHM), Maui: 30 minutes

Molokai Airport (MKK), Molokai: 20 minutes

Lanai Airport (LNY), Lanai: 25 minutes

Hilo International Airport (ITO), island of Hawaii: 50 minutes

Ellison Onizuka Kona International Airport at Keahole (KOA), island of Hawaii: 45 minutes

The airports on the islands of Molokai and Lanai are limited to commuter airlines, as are the two smaller airports on Maui: Kapalua Airport and Hana Airport. In addition, there is daily ferry service from Lahaina Harbor on Maui to Manele Bay on Lanai.

Visas

All international visitors, regardless of country of origin, must present a valid passport or secure document when entering the United States, including Hawaii. As of this writing, it may be possible COVID documents will also be needed. Although not necessary for US citizens, a passport certainly makes your entry go more smoothly.

TRAVEL. STATE. GOV is an excellent resource for in-depth information on types of visitor visas. For more specific information on entering U. S. borders, please review the U. S. Dept. of Homeland Security's website.

The Visa Waiver Program enables nationals of 38 participating countries to travel to the United States for tourism or business for stays of 90 days or less without obtaining a visa. All travelers

Reeling in the big one... sportfishing is a popular pastime in the Hawaiian Islands.

Enjoying the spray at the base of Wailua Waterfall, near Hana, Maui.

entering under this program are required to have a valid authorization through the Electronic System for Travel Authorization (ESTA) prior to travel. See U. S. Customs and Border Protection's frequently asked questions.

Customs

Flying to Hawaii is different than traveling to many other US and worldwide destinations. According to the Hawaii Biological Survey, Hawaii is the "endangered species capital of the world," with more endangered or threatened species per square mile than any other place on the planet.

Bringing non-native species of plants and animals into Hawaii state can cause harmful effects on human health and well-being, agriculture and Hawaii's fragile native ecosystem. As a result, the State of Hawaii Department of Agriculture requires passengers arriving with plants, seeds, animals and any other agricultural materials to declare them on the Agricultural Declaration Form distributed aboard your flight to Hawaii. Plant quarantine inspectors will be stationed in the baggage claim area to examine baggage and agricultural items.

There is also an optional survey passengers may fill out on the back side of the form. Please "kokua" (help) in protecting the unique environment, agriculture and communities.

Clothing

In Hawaii, every day feels like Aloha Friday. Clothing is casual, and except for one or two upscale restaurants, jackets are not required for dinner. Men in Hawaii have it easy because aloha shirts (casual button-down or collared shirts) are appropriate for just about any occasion. Hawaii's year-round tropical climate ranges from bikini weather during the day to a light sweater or jacket in the evening. Comfortable shoes or sandals are fine for most occasions.

If you will be hiking or will require specialty clothing/equipment, consider buying your gear before you arrive, as the selection can be limited on some islands. A light jacket is recommended for wind and rain. This is especially important if you will be spending lengthy amounts of time on the summits of Haleakala on Maui or Maunakea on the island of Hawaii, or camping in higher elevations like Upcountry Maui or Hawaii Volcanoes National Park.

Accommodations

Many resorts and hotels can be found around Waikiki on Oahu. You can also find luxury resorts in east Honolulu, on the North Shore and on the Leeward Coast in the Ko Olina Resort area. On the other islands there are resort areas that are entities unto themselves along with small towns that support a variety of accommodations. AirBnBs have become very popular throughout the state where you can find full homes, actual bed and breakfast establishments and privately owned condos in resorts. Hawaii has become so popular that it is not recommended to arrive without a reservation. For many parts of the year, last minute accommodations can prove to be very expensive. Inquire with your dive operator. Most can give you recommendations on where to stay to fit your budget and also avoid long drives early in the morning to board your charter.

Safety & Security

Given its unique structure and variety, Hawaii is a remarkably safe society. As is the case everywhere in the world, in places where tourists gather, be aware that others also gather there to prey on tourists and be vigilant of your belongings. Waikiki is rumbling along at over a million people now, so it is a big city. Act accordingly and be safe. There is no state police in Hawaii. Each of the four counties in the state is responsible for its own police force. For health or criminal emergencies, call 911.

Money

You are in the United States and so just like the mainland, all US dollar amenities are available. Not all banks will exchange foreign currency so check with them first. If you don't use dollars where you live, it is helpful to exchange some of your currency before you travel so you'll have US money for cab fare (Uber and Lyft are available too) and other incidentals. International ATM (automated teller machine) service signs display on the machines the logos of usable credit cards. The ATMs can be found nearly everywhere.

Health

Each year, Hawaii welcomes millions of visitors from around the world. Like any destination, health risks are preventable with awareness and a few precautions. Medical systems and facilities in Hawaii are well-established, so you can expect to receive a high standard medical treatment, should you have a problem with your health during your stay. Necessary drugs can be purchased at drugstores as long as you have a doctor's prescription. Be aware of any natural and human-caused hazards as well as health emergencies and threats, like COVID-19. Plan your vacation accordingly and take proper precautions before you leave. Also, make sure your insurance is accepted in Hawaii, if not, buy travel insurance.

When visiting a farmer's market, roadside produce stand, local farm or home garden, make sure to thoroughly rinse all fruits and vegetables under clean, running water, especially leafy green produce. Check single leaves of leafy vegetables for tiny slugs and snails, which can carry parasites that cause rat lungworm disease, a severe form of meningitis. If you plan to eat snails, freshwater prawns, crabs, or frogs, boil them for at least 3-5 minutes to kill any parasites.

Check with your dive shop concerning the whereabouts of the nearest diving recompression chamber. Check with lifeguards for current conditions and obey all posted warning signs. Hawaii's oceans have high surf and strong riptides that are hazardous even for experienced swimmers. Knowing your limits and respecting the ocean could save your life. Stay out of the shore break where waves break abruptly in shallow water. Always "duck dive" under oncoming or crashing waves with arms held in front of your head to avoid injury and allow the wave to roll over you.

Hawaii is prone to invasions of box jellyfish, which can deliver a painful sting. Stay out of the water when warning signs are posted. Seek immediate medical attention if you've been stung and have difficulty breathing or problems with vision, cramps, or heart palpitations.

Don't go swimming after heavy rains. Bacteria levels may be higher than normal due to increased runoff. If you do choose to go swimming, cover any open cuts or wounds and practice good hygiene by thoroughly rinsing off afterwards. Keep cuts and scrapes clean and covered with a bandage until healed to prevent infections from dirt and bacteria, such as Staphylococcus aureus (staph). If you have an open wound, stay out of freshwater streams, areas where freshwater and seawater mix (brackish water), waterfalls, or other waters under an advisory on exposure to bacterial diseases.

Hawaii is home to some of the world's most beautiful and adventurous hiking trails. Use only maintained sanctioned trails. Vog, or "volcanic fog," is the hazy air pollution caused by volcanic emissions from volcanoes like Kilauea on Hawaii Island. If you have a pre-existing respiratory condition, keep

Sunset along the Kona coast

A zigzag portion of the road just past the Ulupalakua area on the Backside Route to Hana, Maui.

your medication available and use as prescribed. To protect yourself from vog, be aware of wind conditions that may carry vog to your area.

Insurance

Most common ailments can be treated locally, but you should ensure you have DAN insurance or similar medical and evacuation coverage before coming to Hawaii to dive.

As always, the best way for divers to avoid decompression illness is to dive conservatively and well within the guidelines set by your computer, maintain slow ascent rates and keep well hydrated pre-dive and post-dive. If you do think you might be bent, **contact DAN Emergency +1-919-684-9111 International Emergency Hotline.**

The doctor at the end of the phone will give you advice whether you are a DAN member or not and, to our mind, this in itself is a powerful reason to support such an excellent organization. But, be aware, if you do not have DAN insurance, DAN will not pay your medical or evacuation expenses, nor will your dive operator. Carry insurance... you know it makes sense.

Communication

Hawaii is well-wired for communication with WiFi and cell services. If you want a SIM card for your phone, the main carriers are Verizon, T-Mobile or AT&T. They sell in their company stores SIM cards for U. S. prepaid assistance. The area code for the state of Hawaii is (808).

Time

Keeping time straight is easy here as all of Hawaii is in the same time zone, which is 10 hours ahead of G. M. T. Daylight Saving Time is not practiced in Hawaii. Except for most of Arizona, it is the only state in the United States that does not use DST at all.

Breaching humpback whale

A rainbow in Kalalau Valley at sunset.

A red tailed tropic bird and Kalalau Valley at sunset, Kauai.

KAUAI

Each of the Hawaiian Islands has more than one name, Kauai is also known as The Garden Isle and as the name implies it is indeed lush and green. It holds the distinction of having a location that is, in most years, the wettest on the planet. Nearly 500in (1270cm) of rain drops annually on Mount Waialeale. At 8 million years old, Kauai is the elder of the main islands and the most eroded.

Large rivers have cut spectacular canyons through the green mountains to create breath taking scenery, much of which can only be accessed by helicopter tours and there are many companies to choose from should you decide on this opportunity. From land the Grand Canyon of the Pacific,

Waimea Canyon, is accessible by car through Koke'e State Park. This volcanic wonder is over a mile wide, nearly 4000ft (1202m) deep and ten miles (16km) long. The other spectacular view by car is found on the opposite side of the island, Hanalei Valley. Over 900 acres have been set aside here as a National Wildlife Refuge. There is a spectacular highway view from above the valley and the road then meanders down through fields of taro and on into the charming little town of Hanalei.

The oldest reefs here have created the most miles of beaches of all the main islands and some spectacular shore diving and snorkeling. The pre-eminent dive site on the north shore is Tunnels. Most dive shops have guides

Tunnel of Trees road leads to
the Poipu area of Kauai.

Waterfall on the island of Kauai

available to escort you for shore diving, which is well worth it because they will bring your gear to the entry point on the beach. Also, going in and out of the many lava tubes, tunnels and arches can be disorienting so it is best to have a guide who knows the way so you won't get lost during your undersea adventure.

Kauai is home to a variety of outdoor activities. You can kayak the Wailua River, snorkel on Poipu Beach, hike the trails of Kokee State Park or go ziplining above Kauai's lush valleys.

The Na Pali coast of Kauai is one of the most dramatic — and dangerous — coastlines in all of the Pacific. And the daunting Kalalau Trail hugs its rugged back along 11mi (17.5km) of muddy paths where one wrong step could be your last. For the truly adventurous, a permit from the park rangers lets you hike the entire way to Kalalau Beach, where a "Fantasy Island" waterfall and starlit night skies await. For the rest of us, a 4mi (6.5km) round trip gets you to Hanakapiai Beach, where a cool, freshwater stream will refuel you for the return trip. But, it is the island's laid-back atmosphere and rich culture found in its small towns that make it truly timeless. Exploring the various regions of Kauai, both accessible and ruggedly hidden, is part of the undeniable allure of the island.

The Best of Kauai

1) **Brennecke's Ledge**
2) **Prince Kuhio Park**
3) **Koloa Landing**
4) **Sheraton Caverns**
5) **Turtle Bluffs**
6) **Amber's Arches**
7) **Tunnels**
8) **Kilauea Arch**

Gray reef shark

1) Brennecke's Ledge
Location: SE Kauai
Depth: 60-80ft (18-25m)

B renneke's Ledge is located at the east end of Kauai's south side dive sites. It is often done as a drift dive due to strong and changing currents that can be found here. It is also a large area and can be done as more than a single dive. In the many cuts in the wall, you'll see the antenna of lobsters test the passing flow and the cup corals open during the day to take advantage of the water movement.Large antler corals are swarmed by clouds of Hawaiian whitespot damsels as divers pass by. A school of blue stripe snapper, locally referred to as ta'ape, will retreat from midwater to the reef as bubbles approach. Deeper down trees of black coral are home to tiny gobies and, occasionally, longnose hawkfish.

The site also holds the promise of seeing a type of fish that is not usually seen this far east in the state. The Spotted Knifejaw (*Oplegnathus punctatus*), reaching up to 28in (.7m), can sometimes be seen in the main Hawaiian Islands, most often around Kauai and Niihau. It is most always only encountered at the very northernmost end of our State, from Pearl and Hermes Atoll to Midway and Kure Atolls. Their fused beaklike teeth are adapted for crushing the shells of mollusks which is a favorite food for these fish along with algae. Two species occur in Hawaii, the Barred Knifejaw (*Oplegnathus fasciatus*) being much more rare than the Spotted. Look into the blue for a possible shark or whale, but small stuff is also great. There are eels and lots of inverts, even harlequin shrimp, to observe and photograph at Brenneke's Ledge.

Humpback calf

Whitemouth Moray Eel and
slate pencil sea urchin.

33

Paddler boarder and green sea turtle in the shallows

2) Prince Kuhio Park
Location: Offshore of the park
Depth: 10-50ft (3-16m)

Prince Kuhio Park is a great shallow warm-up dive where you can see green sea turtles. The sandy beach can be seasonal and washed away by the large south swells in the summer. If there are surfers out, it is probably best to pick another location. Regardless, the entry is rocky so it is best to wear a thin wetsuit for protection from bumping into the abrasive lava. A boat dive here will avoid the trials of the rocky entry.

On most days you will be rewarded with 100ft (30m) visibility and six to twenty turtles. To the right, as you are looking out, is a cleaning station. The turtles will pose for pictures as they are very used to snorkelers and divers. This area is fairly protected and home to a smattering of fish life and especially some juveniles that hide in the corals and cracks. Look for spotted boxfish babies, tangs and, at night, amusing boxer crabs. Tanks are available at Seasport Divers just down the road in Poipu. Tell Marvin we say Aloha.

Endemic Hawaiian pom-pom crab or boxer crab with anemones it carries around and uses for defense

Seeing sea turtles is
a given at Prince Kuhio

Kanoe Lani Dodd sporting a head lei or haku.

The HULA

Mention Hawaii and everyone thinks of beautiful hula dancers. Hula is a Polynesian dance form accompanied by chant (oli) or song (mele). It was developed in the Hawaiian Islands by the Polynesians who originally settled there. The hula dramatizes or portrays the words of the oli or mele in a visual dance form. There are many sub-styles of hula, with the main two categories being Hula ʻAuana and Hula Kahiko. Ancient hula, as performed before Western encounters with Hawaii, is called kahiko. It is accompanied by chant and traditional instruments. Hula, as it evolved under Western influence in the 19th and 20th centuries, is called ʻauana (a word that means "to wander"

or "drift"). It is accompanied by song and Western-influenced musical instruments such as the guitar, the ukulele and the double bass.

Traditional female dancers wore the everyday pāʻū, or wrapped skirt, but were topless. Today this form of dress has been altered. Dancers might also wear decorations such as necklaces, bracelets and anklets, as well as many leis and other accessories.

Traditional male dancers wore the everyday loincloth. The materials for the lei were gathered in the forest. This was preceded by prayers and chants to Laka and the forest gods. The lei and tapa worn for sacred hula were imbued with the holiness of the dance and were not to be worn after the performance.

Hawaiian hula dancers
© Hawaii Tourism Authority

Whitetip shark and
bigscale soldierfish

Looking down on the landing entry (Apple Maps)

3) Koloa Landing
Location: Hanaka'ape Bay
Depth: 20-50ft (6-15m)

This is one of the easiest shore dives on the island and usually safe due to lack of surf, surge and currents. If surgy, take extra care and enter slowly, watching your step. There is a state mooring in 30ft (9m) of water so listen for boats and try not to surface offshore. It is also a popular training area and great spot to spend a lot of time underwater for photographers. The landing was Kauai's main harbor many years ago and an old boat ramp is still present. It can be slippery. Walk down carefully for easy entry.

Dive on the left or right of the entry. Depths here max out at about 50ft (15m) but there are things to see in even shallower depths. If you are lucky, you will see some passing or resting whitetip reef sharks at Koloa Landing. Stubby finger corals grow on top of the many

rocks on either side of the bay where schooling snapper can be found. Raccoon butterflyfish are commonly seen as are graceful trumpetfish that are out hunting for a snack. Look also for groupings of Moorish idols atop the coral stands.

The center sandy area is good for peacock flounders and shy freckled snake eels who gulp to pump water through their gills. Green sea turtles and even the Hawaiian monk seal make appearances here. Nice long dives can be made here producing plenty of photos or videos. Many divers bring two tanks and make a full morning of it.

Raccoon butterflyfish

Diver, blue striped snappers and a green sea turtle at Sheraton Caverns.

The gold lace nudibranch, Halgerda terramtuentis, is found in rocky areas and caves around Hawaii.

4)Sheraton Caverns
Location: South side of Kauai
Depth: 35-60ft (10-18m)

Giant striding into the clear waters off the Sheraton Kauai Resort will put you in the busy world of sea turtles, lava tubes and tropical fish. Sheraton Caverns is said to be Kauai's signature dive, a fact that is backed up by the placement of five state moorings for charter operators. This is one of the few dives around the island where you are likely to be joined by another boatload of divers and there is good reason for this. Three large lava tubes form a "Y" shape with plenty of room for divers. Light filters in through numerous locations but you will need your own light to really get the most out of this site. Two cracks house spiny lobsters and slipper lobsters can be found almost anywhere inside. Up on the ceiling lives an endemic nudibranch, the gold-lace nudibranch (*Halgerda terramtuentis*), which is sometimes dislodged with divers' bubbles.

Sections inside are covered with cup coral which open at night like a bouquet of flowers. This is only one of many reasons to night dive here. Whitetip reef sharks sleep here during the day, although too many divers will cause them to vacate the area for an hour or two, so it is best to get here early. Yellowmargin and whitemouth moray eels are easily seen poking their heads out of their homes and even scurrying over the reef. It will take a light and probably a dive guide to locate the viper moray that curls up far back into crevices. Commerson's

Viper moray eel

frogfish frequent this site along with a school of surgeonfish that can be found milling about outside the caverns with blue-striped snapper nearby.

Photographers will be hard-pressed to choose between a wide angle lens or macro. Archways and canyons here make dramatic frames for silhouettes of divers. The solution is to dive here more than once.

The advantage of shooting at a site that is frequented by divers is that the marine life here is much more tolerant of large cameras with twin strobes. Fish that are difficult to approach on most sites can fill your viewfinder

here. In the winter, the sound of humpback whales singing can be so loud you would expect to look out into the blue and see them. Passing whales have been spotted more than once, but it is rare. Spinner dolphins traversing the site are more likely and this can occur year 'round. Although it can be shore dived, a boat dive is by far easiest and safest in all but the calmest conditions.

Whitetip sharks

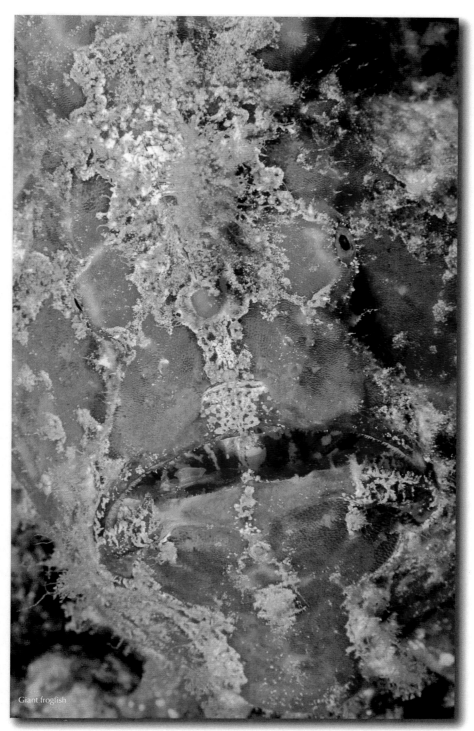

Giant frogfish

Diver watches two green sea turtles at Turtle Bluffs

5) Turtle Bluffs
Location: 1/4 mile south from Manoloa
Depth: 40-90ft (13-30m)

Turtle Bluffs is a favorite boat dive with pretty much guaranteed sea turtles. The state mooring is attached to a pin at 60ft (18m) and this is likely where you will begin. The site has a number of plateaus surrounding a mound that tops off around 45ft (13m). Here green sea turtles congregate to be cleaned by surgeonfish and wrasse. The bottom slopes offshore to 65ft (19m) and then drops to 90 (27m). Whitetip reef sharks sleep here until disturbed by

Hawaiian morwong

Photographing a green sea turtle

divers. If you sit patiently still, the sharks will likely return shortly to their favored resting spot.

For fish lovers, this has a real bonus as Hawaiian morwongs have been spotted in small congregations here. These odd fish have thick reddish lips and bold diagonal black stripes which may serve to disrupt their outline or to make them appear extra large to predators. Bony lumps and bumps adorn the front of the head. They often prop themselves on the bottom with strong pectoral fins, somewhat like hawkfishes. Divers on Kauai and along Oahu's north shore have perhaps the best chance of seeing them. But that's not all. Very cooperative boarfish are sometimes seen under an archway. Resembling oversized Moorish idols with whiskers, they are very rare to see around the main islands. Occasionally glance up into the water column for passing pelagics. Leave it to your charter captain to pick an alternate site if the current is running here. This spot is best experienced when the current is light to non-existant.

Longnose hawkfish

6) Amber's Arches
Location: 1/4 mile SE of Puolo Point off the Port Allen Airport
Depth: 45-75ft (13-23m)

Amber's Arches begins at the state mooring pin in 45ft (13m) of water. A short kick over to the dropoff reveals ledges and archways that tumble past 70ft (21m). A light and some patience will reveal longnose hawkfish in one of the black coral trees at the deep end of your dive. On the way down look for lobster antennaes moving under the ledges like the baton of an orchestra conductor. Look also for bicolor anthias searching the current for a bite to eat. You can zigzag back through structures with sizable openings good for several divers. The big arch has a large school of ta'ape that will hang in midwater. Colonial cup corals decorate the shadows. One section is home to Hawaiian sergeant majors that have interbred with a relatively new species to the state, the Indo-Pacific sergeant major. Marine biologists are arguing about the consequences of this possibly new species, since the endemic Hawaiian sergeant major is thought to have original ties to this Indo-Pacific species. Discussions and DNA investigations will be ongoing.

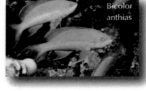
Bicolor anthias

A bluefin jack (ulua) swims through
school of raccoon butterflyfish

Diver swimming through a lava canyon

7) Tunnels
Location: Kauai North Shore, Ha'ena State Park, nine-tenths of a mile past the 8 mile marker
Depth: 15-115ft (4-27m)

If you like weaving your way through lava tubes and poking a light into caves, this is the shore dive for you. There are a few caveats... **1)** get to the parking area early in the morning or you will not get a spot and will end up having to carry your gear a long distance (and avoid the weekends altogether). **2)** a local guide is worth his/her weight in gold. You will see and

Cruising eagle ray

experience much more with someone who knows the reef like his/her backyard. **3)** Forget this place in the winter. The same huge swells that hit Oahu's famous surfing spots hit here as well, so this is a summertime location. **4)** Current can be a factor here so plan accordingly. **5)** There can be boat traffic so make your way up into the shallows at the end of your dive and avoid surfacing offshore.

If you ignore #2, look for a light colored sand channel break in the lava shoreline to enter, put your fins on in waist-deep water and then make your way out. Some of the lava tubes begin in 20ft (6m) of water. Start there and then meander your way towards 60ft (18m). Four dives out of five you will see whitetip reef sharks here and many have reported seeing them being cleaned. Turtles sleep back in a few of the caves and your dive guide should have a light so you can easily get a good look at one.

If you have one, bring it as well or ask your guide in advance to bring a spare. Eels with cleaner shrimp nearby are usually in one cave.

Out on the reef you will see triggerfish, parrotfish and possibly leaf scorpionfish. The latter are often yellowish green even red ones have been observed here. This is a large area and even with a second tank you will not see it all.

Moray eel being cleaned by a banded coral shrimp

Mokuaeae Island

8) Kilauea Arch
Location: Mokuaeae Is. off Kilauea Pt.
Depth: 30-110ft (10-34m)

Mokuaeae Island is a bird sanctuary and part of the Kilauea Point National Wildlife Refuge. Off the north side of the island at 60ft (18m) you will hit the top of Kilauea Arch which drops down to 110ft (33m) where you will find a series of caves. No charter boats are operating trips here at the time of this writing so you can count yourself as extremely lucky if you experience this wild section of reef.

Immediately underwater you can tell that you are somewhere different. Soft octocorals blanket areas up in the shallows and deeper down lobster walk about unaccustomed to

Yellow trumpetfish, squirrelfish and soldierfish

Hawaiian monk seal

intruders. Look also for tiger, reticulated and mole cowries. Schools of surgeonfish fill the water column with large jacks moving in groups like a pack of wolves.

Several species of sharks patrol the depths and spinner dolphins pass by on a regular basis. Back in the boat look for monk seals pulled out on the rocky shoreline to warm in the sun. There will be several species of seabirds working the sky above including red and white tailed tropic birds who make their home on the cliffs.

This area is pounded by surf on most days and even moreso in the winter. Watch the weather in the spring and fall for a prediction of several days of light and variable winds. Even then, cross your fingers too.

Monk seal and green sea turtle warming up on the sand.

Monk Seals

Hawaiian monk seals are the most endangered marine mammal in US waters. There numbers have declined steadily for the last twenty years and much work is being done in an attempt to reverse this trend. They were common on all the islands before man arrived, but since that time they have slowly been forced up to the remote atolls in the Northwestern Hawaiian Islands. The reefs in these areas provide the lobsters, octopus, moray eels and reef fish that make up their diet. But they do occasionally wander down to the eastern islands, so you may get lucky and see one sunning on the beach or zipping by as you dive or snorkel.

An adult monk seal pushes 600 pounds and has quite an appetite. In the past decade, a few individuals have made their home around all of the main islands and quite a few births have been recorded, particularly around Kauai. The more remote areas north of Kauai and around Niihau and Lehua Rocks are sites where they have been seen. They even come to greet divers when they are feeling playful.

Factors that threaten these rare mammals include: interaction and competition with fishing ventures; entanglement in marine debris such as large fishing nets; shark attack and conflict with other monk seals during mating season.

They may look awkward when you see them on land but they are excellent and powerful swimmers in the water and a pleasure to watch. They are great photo subjects of you can get them to pose for you underwater, often mugging

Monk seal mugs for the camera

for the camera. But normal "in the wild" monk seals almost never attack or seek interactions with humans.

Both on land and underwater, these seals are federally protected so don't approach them or harass them. You could wind up getting fined. Photograph them from a respectful distance and don't interfere in what they are doing... just enjoy the rare sighting.

Encounters with Hawaiian monk seals (endemic and endangered) are few and far between. Here a monk seal shares a patch of sand on a Maui roadside with tourists.

Lehua Rock, a tuft crater/seabird sanctuary west of Kauai.

NIIHAU AND LEHUA ROCK

A wisened hand of many decades of Hawaii diving said that "Niihau is one of the last untouched frontiers in the Hawaii Islands, and the diversity of the marine life and the geography is unlike any other."

The westernmost island in the chain, which is about 17mi (27km) from Kauai across the Kaulakahi Channel, is privately owned and off-limits to tourists. Getting here and also to Lehua Rock and making some dives is truly an adventure, but, at times, it can be not for the faint of heart! These are considered some of Kauai's more advanced dives but the reward for the effort can mean an amazing day. The sites promise clear waters, brisk drift dives, deep reefs and awesome structures that, with any luck, should bring in some of Kauai's most elusive and sought-after creatures.

Niihau and Lehua offer incredible diving with over 11 sites total to choose from. It takes a lot of cooperation from the weather. Trips are not done here all the time. But if you get a chance, a lot can happen as these islands are pretty much the realm of the fish and the marine mammals. There is always promise of challenging and exciting dives when you enter these waters. The sites are usually gin clear and just about anything big including marine mammals like whales, dolphins and monk seals can make an appearance. Large sharks can show up so look into the blue on these dives.
Here are two of our favorites.

Best of Nihau & Lehua

9) Keyhole
10) Pyramid Point

A school of bigeye jacks

9) Keyhole
Location: Outside NW tip Lehua Rock
Depth: 15-60-130ft (4-18-40m)

This site is named more for the topside topography as there is an awesome lava rock formation resembling a giant's keyhole. The crack continues underwater and then a wall drops to a cave at 130ft (40m). One of our last dives here was to photograph a rare anthias that can only be seen at depth on two sites around Maui. Since the last two bleaching episodes in 2014 and 2015 and the unusual warming of the water, it seems likely this species has dropped deeper to a more comfortable temperature. The black coral tree is here with longnose hawkfish.

This dive is normally done as a drift dive going either north towards Lehua Gardens or south to Pyramid Point depending on the current direction. Expect numerous sightings of gray reef sharks patrolling the blue and whitetip reef sharks. Large schools of jacks, unheard of around the main islands, cruise many of the stunning sites here.

You'll know when you have made it to Lehua Gardens by the vast fields of leather coral and look for vertical lava tubes that begin at 25ft (7.5m) and drop to 65 (19m). In the other direction at Pyramid Point, you end up in the namesake school of pyramid butterflyfish. A protected ledge up shallow is a great place to spend your safety stop. Look for octopus here.

The Keyhole formation

This deepwater anthias (endemic - Odontanthias fuscipinnis) was first identified with submersibles. To this date only a handful of photographers have had the chance to record this species.

10) Vertical Awareness
Location: SW Corner of Lehua Rock
Depth: 40-120ft (12-36m)

You could roll out a football field at 40ft (12m) on the flat top of this seamount with room to spare. One side of the pinnacle is a vertical drop to nearly 300ft (90m). Large black coral trees can be found just below 100ft (30m) with several species of anthias nearby. A narrow canyon cuts through a section and is often filled with schooling jacks. The same school can also be found in midwater between Lehua and the pinnacle.

Over the centuries, rock-boring urchins have carved a vast convoluted web of three-inch corridors in the hard

A friendly monk seal

A look at the sloping backside of the crescent shaped Lehua Island,

volcanic surface leaving a memorable design behind. Monk seals frequent the site along with Galapagos sharks, eagle rays and there are schools of opelu (small mackerel) being herded by tuna. Pyramid butterflyfish like to hang along walls and they school in the currenty areas. This is a meandering drift dive, with the direction often dictated by what you encounter, so stick with your guide and be prepared for an open water safety stop. Beaked whales and dolphins can be seen at open sea. With luck, they may join the dive boat.

Black coral in the foreground and sharks above

Sunset on the city off Honolulu

OAHU

Oahu is the home of Hawaii's largest city, Honolulu, Waikiki Beach, Diamond Head and Pearl Harbor. It is the third largest island but it holds over 75% of the state's population, which is growing. This is where virtually everyone enters the state at Inouye International Airport (HNL), also called Honolulu International Airport (again everything in Hawaii seems to have two names).

The city itself is now topping over a million people, so it can be a bit congested, especially at rush hour. Oahu has been referred to as a big city with a beach, but there is much, much more here than just the city. Although, if you are looking for nightlife after your dives, this is the island. You will be hard-pressed in the rest of the state to find much going on late in the evening.

There is plenty to do in the city during the day as well. The Waikiki Aquarium can acquaint you with Hawaiian marine life and there is even a sprawling Zoo nearby. There is no end to dining possibilities here in the big city and we would steer you to a personal favorite, Chai's Island Bistro in front of the Aloha Tower Marketplace.

If you have some non-divers in your party wanting to get hands on with the ocean, head out to Sea Life Park on the east side of Oahu. They have a supervised dolphin encounter and you can even go underwater into their reef tank with a bubble helmet and feed eagle rays and turtles. The other "do not miss" adventure, regardless of if you dive or not, is a shark cage snorkel off Hale'iwa Town on Oahu's North Shore. Hawaii Shark Encounters was started by the late Jimmy Hall, who tragically passed away in May 2007 in an

Waikiki bay area with
Diamond Head in the distance
©HTA / Vincent Lim

Sharks far off Oahu's
North Shore

creatures have no interest in biting people and are just there for the free meal. Their fluid movement and natural power is mesmerizing and your fear melts away when you realize you are looking at 500,000 million years of evolution swimming majestically by. The tour is fun and educational with plenty of shark materials to read. This is also the area where the immense waves roll into the North Shore. If you're lucky, a surfing tournament will be taking place. Sometimes jawdroppingly huge waves roll in.

accident north of the Arctic Circle. Those who took over Jimmy's company run cages three miles out into open ocean to experience Galapagos and sandbar sharks up close. This is a surface cage for snorkelers who go inside and safely peer out through a plexiglass window to see the sharks swimming by.

If the conditions are on your side it is well worth the trip for anyone who would like to overcome a fear of sharks. These fish come to the boat for bait and it is obvious after your first minute in the water that these magnificent

The Best of Oahu

11) **Hanauma Bay**
12) **Turtle Canyon**
13) **Baby Barge**
14) **Corsair Plane**
15) **YO-257 and**
San Pedro Wrecks
16) **The Sea Tiger Wreck**
17) **The Mahi Wreck**
18) **Electric Beach**
19) **Haleiwa Trench**
20) **Three Tables**
21) **Shark's Cove**
22) **Moku Manu**

Oahu coastal highway
©HTA / Vincent Lim

Schooling endemic millet seed butterflyfish (Chaetodon miliaris).

A State of Isolation

The eight main islands that make up the State of Hawaii are some of the most isolated fragments of land in all the world. Neatly centered in the middle of the largest ocean on our planet, these reefs were challenged to host any life whatsoever. Besides just distance, the dominant currents that sweep around the Pacific only rarely come into contact with Hawaiian waters. These currents are the way larval creatures such as fish, corals and mollusks are dispersed. In some cases hundreds of thousands of years passed before a new species found its way to

the islands, and then, there was the problem of locating a mate. This occasionally brought about the existence of a new form of life. The survival time of creatures in this larval state varies from one species to the next. Anemonefish, for example, have a very short time they can survive in open ocean before they must settle to the reef. So there are no anemonefish in Hawaii. To this day approximately 23% of the fish species in Hawaii are endemic. You can dive all over the world, but only in Hawaii will you find these unique individuals. Many can be

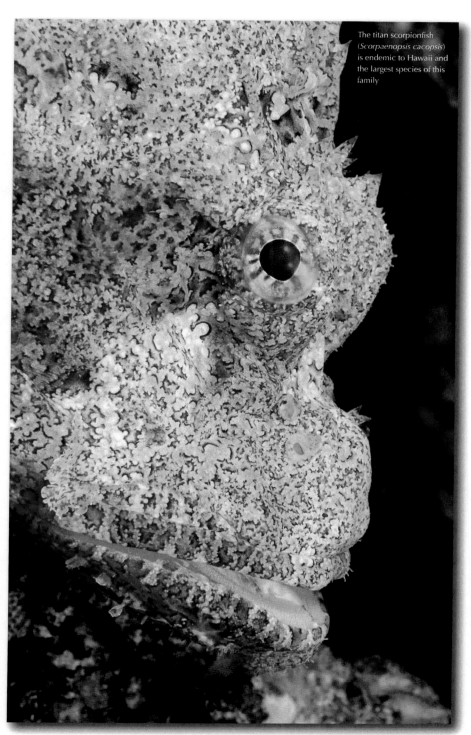

The titan scorpionfish (*Scorpaenopsis cacopsis*) is endemic to Hawaii and the largest species of this family

Potter's angelfish, (*Centropyge potteri*), are found only in Hawaii, where they are the most common representative of this family.

traced back to relatives that are found in the South Pacific, but a few, such as the bandit angelfish (*Apolemichthys arcuatus*), have no close relatives and it is not known how they came to exist. Three of the five angelfish found in Hawaii are endemic. A slightly lesser percentage of mollusks, corals, crustaceans and algae follow the same endemic trend as the fishes.

Indonesia, in the southwest corner of the Pacific Ocean, is thought to be the beginning of life in the seas. Nearly 3000 species of fish have been recorded from it's waters, the most in all the world. No matter what direction you journey in from Indonesia, this number drops. Moving towards Hawaii, Guam is home to 1400 species. At the Marshall Islands, the number drops to 1000. Finally, in Hawaii, 650 different ocean fishes have been found. Initially this relatively straight line was thought to be the path taken by the marine creatures that are now found in the islands. Dispersal of most marine species takes place during their larval stage early in life, when they are at the mercy of the ocean. Those fortunate enough to survive into adulthood then settle to the bottom to begin life on the reef. The greater the distance, the more difficulty a species would have in dispersing itself in adequate numbers to actually take hold in a new area. Some Hawaiian inhabitants though, did not fit this island hopping idea, which lead ichthyologist to look beyond what they refer to as the stepping-stone theory.

A greater knowledge of the Pacific through satellite research has brought a second factor into play. In the northern hemisphere, the prevailing currents that sweep the Pacific move in a clockwise direction; east to west across the equator, then up towards the Philippines and Japan, and back to an easterly flow above Hawaii to then flow down the coast of North America. Although these oceanic currents circle

Endemic Nene or Hawaiian Goose

Hawaii, none actually flow to the islands themselves, with one exception.

Occasionally a current from the north will curl south enough to reach Hawaii. What causes this is unknown, and many years may pass without this occurring, but it is now thought that a large percentage of the marine life in Hawaii has travelled on this intermittent route. Why one species would survive in sufficient numbers to settle in Hawaii and not another, is unclear. The resulting mixture though is unique in many ways. Some species, which are uncommon in the South Pacific, are found in great numbers by divers in Hawaii. This is conceivably due to the absence of a particular predator that did not find its way to the islands.

So if you are looking for something to do on your dives in Hawaii, try identifying the endemic fishes on each dive. This also extends to the land where there are endemic birds like the nene (Hawaiian goose) and animals,

Hanauma Bay

11) Hanauma Bay
Location: southwest of Oahu
Depth: 15-70ft (4-21m)

This bay is the remnant of some of the last volcanic activity for the island of Oahu around 32,000 years ago. It is one of several vents that formed along the southeast shoreline from compressed ash. Violent explosions often occurred launching large volcanic objects which can be seen imbedded in the circular tuft. Over the thousands of years since its formation, erosion has opened the ocean side to form the current crescent bay complete with a white sand beach and rows of palm trees. It is iconic Oahu along with Waikiki Beach, Pearl Harbor and Diamond Head.

The corners protect the inner bay from strong trade winds that blow the tops off the waves just outside the calm interior. The construction in the late '40s of a paved walkway with guide rail and bathrooms turned the site into an attraction that captivated tourists by the thousands. In 1967, it was declared a marine life conservation area and underwater park but it wasn't until the '90s that it was determined that further protections needed to be in place to alleviate damage to the ecosystem.

An education center was added in 2002 and first time visitors are required to watch a short video stressing visitors not interact with the marine life and not touch the corals. To give the fish a break, the area is closed to the public on Tuesdays, Christmas and New Year's Day. The parking is limited so get here early. Bring your wallet for the park entry fee and your C card if you are diving from shore.

Head to the right side of the beach and look for a channel leading through the inner reef area to the outside. This outer reef is home to a protected

Grazing parrotfish

assemblage of fish including many species of parrotfish. They are a sign of a healthy environment that is not found in unprotected areas around the state. Eels are numerous here... their heads can be seen protruding from coral crevices, opening their mouths as they pump water through their gills. Snowflake eels are often seen snaking their way across the bottom in search of a crab dinner. The bottom slopes out to 60-70ft (18-21m) and on your way look for turtles at cleaning stations. They will be seen being serviced by cooperative tangs and passing eagle rays.

Outside both corners of the bay are popular wall dives that require a boat due to the strong currents. If you begin to feel the pull of the water, congratulations, you have travelled quite a distance underwater and now it is time to turn around and head back in. Back on the beach, enjoy the warm sand or take a hike on one of the many trails that lead to scenic points overlooking the bay.

A turtle at
Turtle Canyon

12) Turtle Canyon
Location: Maunalua Bay, Hawaii Kai.
Depth: 20-45ft (6-15m)

This is a great spot for the less experienced diver and a wonderful location for anyone who would like to spend some time around green sea turtles. The only caveat would be that it is a boat dive that is frequented by many operators so there is a good chance you will not be alone. You will most certainly have snorkelers above you waiting for a turtle to come up for a breath. Fingers of lava point to the open ocean and here you will find cracks and overhangs where the turtles rest. While you may not see them, spinner dolphins like this area and you can hear their calls out in the blue as you dive and search for fishes and critters. But do keep an eye out for the occasional appearance by a curious spinner.

Porcupine pufferfish are common here and are used to divers so they may pose for a shot or two before wiggling off. The many rocks and coral heads hold eels, lobsters and occasionally resting whitetips. Stick with your guide and get back to your boat underwater. It is best not to surface away from your vessel due to the boat traffic here.

Giant pufferfish

Galapagos sharks

13) Baby Barge
Location: West of Hawaii Kai
Depth: 60-80ft (18-24m)

Baby Barge and the nearby **Mini Barge** are a couple of very popular wrecks that are part of an array of purpose-sunk wrecks along the Oahu coast created for attracting fish life and captivating divers. Although it is not a long boat ride, the mornings are usually calmer. As the day goes, by tradewinds can make the ride back a bouncy one.

The ever-changing current can be ripping here at times, so descend down the mooring line and get back to it with 1000 PSI just to be on the safe side. The current that continually sweeps this area provides excellent visibility and attracts marine life. Glance up into the blue occasionally to catch a glimpse of a Galapagos shark or two.

The barge has collapsed into itself and no longer provides a wreck penetration experience, but not to worry, there is plenty to see here. Some enormous green sea turtles like to slide into the slots created by the bent plates of steel and a school of goatfish meander from one end to the other.

Streamline your hoses and equipment to make it less likely to catch on the many pieces of protruding steel. A full 3mm wetsuit is a good choice to protect yourself as well. Whitetip reef sharks share spaces with the turtles and there is a cave nearby that is another favorite for these resting sharks. Stick with your dive guide to get here and look for octopus on your way back to the barge.

If the currents aren't prohibitive, the Mini Barge is a short swim away and offers a similar experience. But this is only for times when currents aren't real

Reticulated butterflyfish with soldierfish in the background

strong. You want to be sure you have enough air to get back up the line and make a stop. Be sure to ascend slowly and don't be afraid to go beyond the three minutes for your safety stop, you never know what might swim by.

Scrawled filefish

The Corsair cockpit

14)Corsair Plane
Location: 15 minutes from Hawaii Kai
Depth: 115ft (35m)

There are many reef dives in Oahu, but this island is also known for several wrecks, some purpose-sunk and some not. This plane is one of the nots. The pilot of the WWII Vought F4U Corsair was on a training mission in 1945 when he ran low on fuel and ditched into the ocean just off Hawaii Kai. The impact bent the propeller blades, but the rest of the plane was intact. The pilot in his life jacket was picked up shortly after it sunk.

It rests in an area swept by strong currents that have buried one wing, which likely has kept the plane in one place through several hurricanes. Follow the mooring line down and then it is a short 30-ft (9m) swim to the wreck. The plane isn't big, being about 33ft (10m) long with a 41ft (12.5m) wingspan and single rotary engine.

Yellowmargin moray eels are at home in the cockpit so look carefully before joining them. A school of goatfish are always on patrol and garden eels can be found in a sandy area nearby. Stingrays are very rare in Hawaii. In thousands of dives David says he has encountered one on just five occasions. But, they have been spotted here, so scan the area around the wreck. There is no place shallow to go at the end of the dive so after 15 minutes make your way up the line to your safety stop.

The plane sits alone on a sandy bottom

Sleeping green sea turtles on the YO deck

15) YO-257 & San Pedro Wrecks
Location: W of Diamond Head State Park
Depth: 65-115ft (19-34m)

The wrecks lay west of Diamond Head State Park
©HTA / Vincent Lim

There are many wreck dives around the island of Oahu, but this is the one you want to put on the top of your list. Atlantis Submarines is responsible for the intentional sinking of both these wrecks. "YO" is the Navy designation for Yard Oiler, which was its purpose for many years in Pearl Harbor before the current assignment as an artificial reef.

The 175ft (53m) long YO went down in 1989 in 115ft (35m), followed by the San Pedro, a 125ft (38m) ex longliner, just in shore around the 85ft (2m) depth in 1996. The two wrecks are close enough to kick from one to the other, but it is not

76

Snappers inside the wreck

recommended due to the strong currents that often occur here. Additionally, Additionally, Atlantis Submarines, with circular ports filled with curious landlubbers, pass regularly in the channel created by the two wrecks. If you have such patrons traveling with you, it is an excellent introduction to the underwater world for those that may never have a chance to experience it on scuba. You will hear the submarines long before you see them and your dive guide will have wisely told you not to approach.

Instead search the large openings cut in the hull that are framed with snowflake coral and look for the largest pufferfish you have ever seen, resting whitetip reef sharks, eels, sponge crab and green sea turtles. When the current is running, look out to the blue on the open ocean side of the YO. Mantas, eagle rays, gray reef and hammerheads sharks, dolphin and even whales have been seen passing by. The San Pedro is a good choice for those looking for a bit more bottom time. The wheelhouse and deck have begun to

collapse inward, making any extensive penetration not recommenced. Gloves are generally frowned upon in Hawaii, but these wreck dives with their many sharp sections of steel are an exception. Both wrecks have decks in the 55-65ft (17-20m) range. Allow for a safety stop before drifting back to the boat. You are directly off the famous Waikiki Beach so do not come up away from your vessel.

Upper deck of the YO-257

The Attack on Pearl Harbor

Pearl Harbor is the U.S. naval base near Honolulu, Hawaii, that was the scene of a devastating surprise attack by Japanese forces on December 7, 1941. Just before 8 a.m. on that Sunday morning, hundreds of Japanese fighter planes descended on the base, where they managed to destroy or damage nearly 20 American naval vessels, including eight battleships, and over 300 airplanes. More than 2,400 Americans died in the attack, including civilians, and another 1,000 people were wounded. The day after the assault, President Franklin D. Roosevelt asked Congress to declare war on Japan.

President Franklin D. Roosevelt addressed a joint session of the U.S. Congress on December 8, the day after the crushing attack on Pearl Harbor. "Yesterday, December 7, 1941 - a date which will live in infamy - the United States of America was suddenly and deliberately attacked by naval and air forces of the Empire of Japan."

He went on to say, "No matter how long it may take us to overcome this premeditated invasion, the American people in their righteous might will win through to absolute victory.

After the Pearl Harbor attack, and for the first time during years of discussion and debate, the American people were united in their determination to go to war. The Japanese had wanted to goad the United States into an agreement to lift the economic sanctions against them; instead, they had pushed their adversary into a global conflict that ultimately resulted in Japan's first occupation by a foreign power.

Today the attack is commemorated by the USS Arizona Memorial run by the US National Parks Service. The Battleship USS Arizona was bombed on December 7, 1941, about 15 minutes into the Japanese attack on Pearl Harbor, killing 1,177 sailors and Marines.

Today, Arizona rests where she fell, submerged in about 40 feet of water just off the coast of Ford Island.

Designed by Honolulu architect Alfred Preis, the memorial was built in 1962 on top of (but not touching) the sunken USS Arizona. The memorial honors the memory of the crew of the USS Arizona, as well as all the other service members and civilians killed in the attack. A total of 2,341 sailors, soldiers and Marines died as a result of the attack, as well as 49 civilians.

The memorial is located on the southern end of the island of Oahu, Hawaii. It can only be accessed by boat from the Pearl Harbor Visitor Center.

The visitor center is not located on a military base and is accessible to the public, with plenty of free parking. The Pearl Harbor Visitor Center is open seven days a week from 7:00 a.m. to 5:00 p.m. with the exception of some holidays. As it is a gravesite and a memorial, recreational scuba diving is not permitted.

US Navy diver at the USS Arizona Memorial (US National Parks Service)

Bluestripe snapper on the Sea Tiger

16) Sea Tiger Wreck
Location: West of Waikiki
Depth: 80-120ft (26-36m)

This is a former Chinese trading vessel originally named Yun Fong Seong No. 303. The ship was taken in the mid '90s from human traffickers when it was carrying over 90 illegal immigrants intending to try to hide inside the state. It

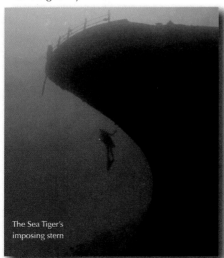

The Sea Tiger's imposing stern

was then bought by Voyager Submarines, cleared inside of equipment and fuel and sunk to create an artificial reef. You can start getting your gear together for this dive when you are still at the dock. It is less than ten minutes to the site from the Kewalo Boat Basin.

At 120ft (35m) to the sandy bottom, this can be a short dive as well, so plan ahead to make the most of it. The main deck is at 90ft (27m) and the only reason to go to the bottom would be if you spotted a Hawaiian stingray or passing eagle ray as you peer over the Sea Tiger's side.

Two large openings in the deck lead to the hold where green sea turtles are often resting in the dark corners, out of sight of tiger sharks that are infrequently seen here. A large school of bluestripe snapper stick close to the wheel house, which is also worth a quick swim-through. The vessel is nearly 170ft (52m) long with two mooring lines. Make sure you end your dive at the one that you descended on to get back to the right boat.

A shoal of bluestripe snapper

Eagle ray squadron

17) The Mahi Wreck
Location: Open water off Waianae
Depth: 10-95ft (3-28m)

The Mahi is a 189ft (63m) minesweeper that was dropped to the bottom as an artificial reef in 1982. That same year Hurricane Iwa turned the entire ship 180°. The bow originally pointed to shore and now faces open ocean sitting upright. Quite an impressive feat of nature to spin an 800 ton vessel. The Waianae Boat Harbor is about a 45 minute drive from Waikiki. On your drive out, once you see the ocean, look for surfers. If there are none you can expect 100ft (30m) visibility on your dive which is a 15-minute boat ride once you depart the harbor.

As you drop down the mooring line you will notice a large percentage of the central deck has collapsed. Working your way into this tangle of steel is not recommended, but peering in with a light might reveal a sleeping whitetip reef shark. Unlike some of the other wreck sites, current here is generally light. If it is running, look just up current for a squadron of pufferfish, the likes of which are rarely found anywhere else.

It is very common to see a group of a dozen or more eagle rays as well. They seem to have a route that regularly takes them around the Mahi. The bottom here is 95ft (29m) and you can spend most of your dive in the 70ft (21m) range to get a bit more bottom time. Eels, schooling goatfish and sergeant majors tending eggs are likely to be seen along with several species of butterflyfish.

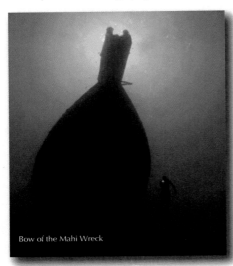
Bow of the Mahi Wreck

Divers descend the line
down to the Mahi Wreck

Spinner dolphins
in the shallows

18) Electric Beach
Location: Kahe Point & Beach Park
Depth: 6-30ft (1.5-9m)

This site is a very popular snorkeling site and also great for photography and long, shallow diving. Another great sea turtle site, divers and snorkelers can also see spinner dolphin pods, whitetip and blacktip reef sharks, schools of endemic sergeant majors and lots of great fish life.

The site at Kahe Point and Kahe Beach Park gets its name from the nearby power plant. This place is out of the city maybe a 45-minute drive in good traffic conditions. The site has submerged exit flow pipes of the power plant that, at this spot, expel warm water into the sea.

This outflow can be strong, so swim away from the pipe openings. Reef fish seem to like warmer water as it attracts schools of parrotfish, damselfish, butterflyfish, surgeonfish and goatfish.

Some beautiful photos of the dolphins and the white sandy bottom have been taken here and there are some small reefs and an old barrier wall (for lack of any other description) that hold coral growth and marine life.

While this is normally done as a beach dive or snorkel, it can also be done by boat. Just remember, you're kind of on your own here with no lifeguards or warning flags at this beach, so only try it when the sea is calm as there can be strong currents and surf when it is rough.

Sea turtle in the sun

Green sea turtle covered in tangs at a cleaning station

19) Haleiwa Trench
Location: North Shore, Oahu
Depth: 20-90ft (6-27m)

Take a scenic trip up north to Haleiwa Beach Park and the site is right offshore. It is best done by boat but can be a shore dive, although there can be a long walk/swim involved to do it all. Local knowledge says this trench is a manmade canyon created to allow submarines to hide. The site is basically a shallow reef flat leading out to a wall that eventually falls down to 90ft (27m). There is a fairly shallow turtle cleaning station here that is a good partial deco stop at the dive's end. This site has plenty of ledges and overhangs that

Gray reef sharks can be seen in the deeper reaches of this site

A puffed up pufferfish

turtles like to rest on... so turtles are plentiful. Look in these same cracks and crevices for cowries, purple urchins and whitemouth morays.

There may be frogfish, snappers and puffers here as well. Down deep you may see grey reef sharks. This site is a popular night dive spot for some of the North Shore dive shops and guides. Look for Spanish dancers to be making their way across the reef. Haleiwa is a great spot to visit and grab something to drink and eat or grab a handmade Hawaiian souvenir.

A mole cowry with the mantle partially covering the shell at night.

Frogfish hiding on an urchin

20) Three Tables
Location: Pupukea Area
Depth: 10-45ft (3-13m)

This is a popular beach for both snorkeling and diving. The small park is named for the three flat rocks out on the close inshore barrier reef that protect the beach a bit. This is not an overly protected site so currents can be strong. Although a popular walk-in dive, boat diving can also be done here so if there are currents, it can be a drift and you can just be picked up. Three Tables is part of the Pupukea Marine Life Conservation District which does not permit fishing here... thus there are healthy and diverse fish populations at Three Tables.

The inner reef flat around the tables and out over the reef is pocked with lava holes and overhangs. Eventually, the reef drops off and the fish viewing begins. There are areas that have nice hard corals and urchins can hold surprises like a camouflaged frogfish.

Lava tubes are on the right side as you face the beach and the dive to the left is a wall dive. Remember, in the winter this area has heavy surf, so shallow corals aren't really that abundant. But, this is really a fishy place so concentrate on the inhabitants as a long dive can be done here. Occasional sightings of sharks coming in are common and the ubiquitous green sea turtles sleep and move along the bottom. Fish that will probably be seen include the humuhumunukunukuapua'a (Picasso triggerfish), whitemouth morays,

The humuhumunukunukuapua'a or Picasso triggerfish

octopus, groups of cornetfish, damsels in the shallows, Moorish idols, hawkfish, parrotfish, unicornfish and the list goes on. If you are a fish person or fish photographer then this is the place for you. This is set up as a little park with tables, restrooms and fresh water to rinse off with, so bring a snack.

Whitemouth moray

Roaming ulua

21) Shark's Cove
Location: Kalalua Point
Depth: 12-80ft (3-24m)

This is another Oahu North Shore dive past Three Tables and also full

Pufferfish eye

of fish life. It is good to note that this is a summer dive as the winter season produces big waves making the site currenty and dangerous. Great for surfers in the Waimea area but not great for divers.This is a good place for snorkeling, beach dives and boat dives, which are the easiest way to go.

There are lots of fish here as this is part of the Pupukea Marine Life Conservation District, so good for underwater photographers

Black triggerfish or durgons are often found in large schools over reef areas.

and snorkelers to capture fish and invertebrate life. Locals joke that Shark's Cove has no sharks. It was apparently named due to the fact that the little bay here is shaped like a shark. But the deeper reaches here may produce a blacktip or whitetip.

If you stay shallow in the 40ft (12m) range, that is where the majority of the fish schools will be. Facing the sea, the left side seems to be the side the fish favor moreso than the right. The site can have currents outside the protection of the bay's ends.

Look for all kinds of fish including many species of surgeonfish, lots of tangs, the marauding bluefin trevallies, trumpetfish and cornetfish, box puffers and the occasional sea turtle. Spend plenty of time looking in the rocks and boulders for flatworms and nudis too. Corals are sparse. Like at Three Tables, this site also has parking and showers.

Millet seed butterflyfish

Cave at Moku Manu

22) Moku Manu
Location: off Makapuu Point
Depth: 60-90ft (18-27m)

Moku Manu, or "Bird Island" in the Hawaiian language, is an islet off the exposed northeast side of Oahu, three-quarters of a mile off Mokapu Peninsula between Kailua and Kaneohe. Moku Manu and an adjacent small islet are connected by an underwater dike. Its highest point is 202ft (62m) high, bordered by near-vertical cliffs on many sides. Moku Manu, like its neighbors to the south, Manana, Kāohikaipu and Mōkōlea Rock, is protected as a state seabird sanctuary. Regardless, landing by boat is nearly impossible due to the lack of a safe beach.

Moku Manu's isolated nature makes it an excellent nesting site. Eleven species of seabirds nest on here, along with several migrating shorebirds. Most days this area is a blown out mess on the surface so you must select one of the rare times this is safe to dive. Spring and fall often have a few days of light winds and a Kona (Southerly) storm system can have one day of shifting directions in which to sneak out as well.

The first thing you will notice underwater is more fish. Isolation has enabled life to flourish here, with one caveat, the creatures are not used to seeing divers so they are difficult to approach. You will see the tail end of many green sea turtles as they swim

Shark silhouetted in a cavern crack

Spinner dolphins in the blue water

away.

The cave pictured (P. 92) on the surface with the boat is a common starting point for most divers. It drops to 90ft (27m) and you will want a light to look for groups of lobster along with several species of moray eels. Deeper inside are a type of shrimp which never see the light of day as well as strange sponges resembling fungi found in old rainforests. Outside, schools of unicornfish pulse over nibbling parrotfish much larger than found elsewhere, picking at coral polyps on the extensive covering of hard corals. The northern islands seaward side has a shallow shelf that drops deep and then really deep into the abyss. It holds a forest of black coral and critters.

Divers can also check the blue for dolphins and pelagics. Most dives here are live boat drifts so bring an inflatable safety marker that you can deploy underwater as you begin your three-minute stop. Strong currents can carry you far from the site in this brief time so a sausage is a necessity.

Northwest Islands

The Northwestern Hawaiian Islands (NWHI) are a chain of tiny islands, atolls and shoals that spans more than 1250mi (2000)km of the north-central Pacific. They stretch from Nihoa Island near Kauai, northwest of the populated Hawaiian Islands, to Kure Atoll, northwest of Midway.

The Northwestern Hawaiian Islands were formed approximately 7-30 million years ago, as shield volcanoes over the same volcanic hotspot that formed the Emperor Seamounts to the north and the main Hawaiian Islands to the south.

As the Pacific Plate moved north and later northwest over the hot spot, volcanic eruptions built up islands in a linear chain. The isolated land masses gradually eroded and subsided, evolving from high islands in the south, much like the main islands of Hawaii, to atolls (or seamounts) north of the Darwin Point. Each of the NWHI are in various stages of erosion.

The largest and hottest shield volcano on Earth was revealed by researchers from the University of Hawaii at Mānoa as we were writing this first edition in 2020. Geoscientists and the public have long thought Mauna Loa, the culturally-significant and active shield volcano on Hawaii Island, was the largest volcano in the world. However, after surveying along the mostly submarine Hawaiian leeward volcano chain, the research team came to a new conclusion. Pūhāhonu, meaning "turtle rising for breath" in Hawaiian, is nearly twice as big as Mauna Loa.

It is known that the ancient Hawaiians ventured from the main islands as far as Mokumanamana (Necker), but they might have gone further to French Frigate Shoals. However, they must have been gone by the 18th century, when Europeans discovered the islands, because the islands were deserted upon discovery. Many agricultural terraces have been found on Nihoa, proving that Hawaiians lived there long-term, but Mokumanamana, with little vegetation, was probably not able to support many people for long. North of the Darwin Point, the land is gradually subsiding more quickly than the coral reef can grow. Kure Atoll straddles the

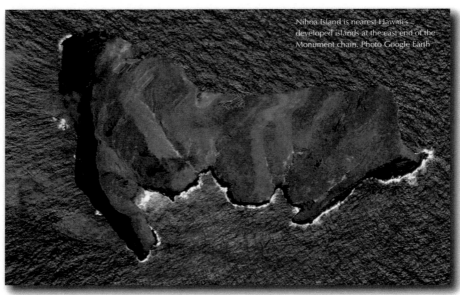

Nihoa Island is nearest Hawaii's developed islands at the east end of the Monument chain. Photo Google Earth

Laysan Island is a refuge for seabirds.
Photo Google Earth

Darwin Point, and will eventually sink beneath the ocean when its coral reef cannot keep up, a destiny that awaits every Hawaiian island.

On June 15, 2006, American President George W. Bush issued a public proclamation creating Papahānaumokuākea Marine National Monument under the Antiquities Act of 1906. The monument encompasses the islands and surrounding waters, forming the largest marine wildlife reserve in the world. President Theodore Roosevelt had declared the Northwestern Hawaiian chain a bird sanctuary in 1909. In August 2016, President Barrack Obama, who visited and snorkeled at Midway Island, expanded the area of the monument by roughly four times. The expanded monument was at that time the world's largest protected area.

No sport diving is allowed up here and entry to the Monument is limited through a permit system. Anyone who comes to the islands must follow strict procedures designed to not disrupt the ecosystem.

Hawaii's Northwest Islands

Kure Atoll
Pearl and Hermes Atoll
Midway Atoll
Pioneer Bank
Lisianski Island
Maro Reef
St. Rogation Bank
Laysan Island
Brooks Banks
Gardner Pinnacles
Necker Island
French Frigate Shoals
Nihoa
Kauai
Niihau
Oahu
Molokai
Lanai
Maui
Kahoolawe
Hawaii (Big Isl)

NORTHWESTERN HAWAIIAN ISLANDS

MAIN HAWAIIAN

MAUI COUNTY

Before divers visit Maui for the first time, they often make the mistake of thinking that it is just one island. Maui County is in fact made up of Maui, Lanai, Molokai and Kaho'olawe. This is the only occurrence of this in the entire state. Returning to Maui from Lanai, on a clear day, you can see the peaks of the Big Island and all four Maui County islands. It is the only place to view five Hawaiian islands at the same time.

You can cross Kahoolawe off your diving list though. In 1941, following Pearl Harbor, the US military used the island as a bombing range until 1990 when President George Bush Sr. ordered an end to the operations.

After an exhaustive but less-than-impeccable $400 million ordinance removal operation, the Kahoolawe Island Reserve was formed which includes the surrounding waters out to two miles (2km). All commercial uses are prohibited, including scuba diving.

Each island in the chain has one or more knick names. Maui, The Valley Isle, was formed over millions of years by two distinct volcanic occurrences. Mauna Kahalewai, a.k.a. the West Maui Mountains was formed by the older of the two volcanic eruptions and this is

Haleakala Volcano Crater

evident in the advanced stage of erosion compared with the younger slopes of the 10,023 ft (3055m) Haleakalā to the south which grew to form the namesake valley connecting the two sides.

This same valley, combined with consistent Northeast trade winds creates an interesting meteorological event known as the Venturi effect.

On a regular "trade wind" day a large area of the waters around Maui can become challenging for vessels and underwater conditions are no better. For this reason a great number of dive boats depart at an early hour, which may have you leaving your hotel before sunrise for a 6 a.m. start.

The advantage of this timetable is that you are often back at the harbor by noon and can participate in some of the many other tours and trips available on an active island like Maui.

While winning many travel industry awards as "Best Island In The World', in recent years concerns have been raised by locals and environmentalists about the overdevelopment of Maui. The island burgeoned into a huge condo and retirement community in the early 2000s. Now, visitors are being urged to be conscious of reducing their environmental footprint while exploring the island. A number of activist groups, including Save Makena have gone as far as taking the government to court to protect the rights of local citizens. But

Maui SUP sunset

the developments and constant tourism have given the island great variety. Eateries, shopping, art and more are found here in great diversity. Like Oahu, traffic can be bad at times, however. So pick your travel times carefully so as not to get bogged down in traffic.

Snorkeling is one of the most popular activities on Maui, with over 30 beaches and bays to snorkel at around the island. And, not all days are blustery, so there are still Plenty of afternoon dive and snorkel choices are available for those who want to do a second beautiful ocean excursion, so their gills do not dry out!

Best Maui County Dives

23) **Molokini - Reef's End**
24) **Molokini - Back Wall**
25) **Puuolai (Red Hill)**
26) **Five Graves**
27) **Olowalu**
28) **The Carthaginian**
29) **Mala Wharf**
30) **Black Rock**

Photographing from a helicopter over the West Maui Mountains

Molokini Crater

23) Molokini - Reefs End
Location: SW Maui
Depth: 15- 76ft (4-23m)

A site that stands out above the others, especially in the media, is Molokini Marine Preserve off South Maui. It is one in a series of vents that run down the side of Haleakala and into the Alalakeiki Channel. Formed from compressed ash, the crescent-shaped islet reaches 160ft (49m) above water. It is a bird sanctuary, so human visitors are not allowed on land. In the summer, nesting frigates take to the sky shortly after dawn.

No matter how good the visibility is along the coastline, it is always better at

Dolphins following the boat

Manta rays are common at Molokini Crater

Molokini. With visibility rarely less than 100ft (30m), sometimes when the planets align visibility can double to 200ft (61m) feet or more. At Reef's End the crater extends underwater, creating a submerged reef a few feet below the surface. A popular area for snorkelers, the crater continues out to the end of the reef, where it then drops off to the surrounding 300ft (91.5m) bottom. Just inside this natural break wall is a sand channel that has historically been the welcome mat for pelagic visitors, including bottlenose dolphin, whale sharks and manta rays. It enjoys a healthy current when it is running and the density of marine life mirrors the passing morsels this provides.

Harlequin shrimp

Slabs of volcanic material form the perfect resting spot for whitetip reef sharks. Most marine life at Molokini is approachable because of the daily encounters with hundreds of divers and snorkelers, so it is a great spot for underwater photographers. Look for dolphins surfing at the boat's bow on the way to and from the site.

Reef octopus doing some acrobatics

24) Molokini - Backwall
Location: Alalakeiki Channel between Maui and Kahoolawe.
Depth: 50-110ft (16-30m)

The outside of the crater, referred to as the Backwall, is an advanced drift dive with no bottom in most sections. A towering 150ft (45m) crater cliff, indented from explosions back when Molokini was used for target practice, drops to over 300ft (91.5m) below the surface, for a jaw-dropping wall drift that can produce some of Hawaii's most sought-after fish and marine mammals.

Molokini is a protected area and designated as a State Marine Life and Bird Conservation District. It is best to dive at 50-80ft (15-24m) letting the current carry you along the wall. Photographers and divers come out here for the chance to see the big stuff. You are likely to see gray reef sharks that occasionally visit a cleaning station where they attempt to vertically hover while Hawaiian cleaner wrasse

Grey reef shark at a cleaning station

Bigeye soldierfish

The Maui Dive Shop boat approaches the Molokini Crater Backwall

inspect them. Frogfish and crevices filled with soldierfish and lobsters keep divers focused on the reef but remember to glance into the blue, where humpback whales inhabit Maui waters from December through March.

If you don't see them, you will definitely hear them singing. A great white shark has even been seen passing by the outside of the crater. Manta rays can be spotted as well. Spinner and bottlenose dolphins may also approach divers, so have your camera ready. After this thrill ride, divers may do a gentler dive inside the crater for a second dive or try one along the Maui coastline.

Breaching humpback male

Hawaii's Whales

Humpback whales, the fifth largest of the great whales, are annual visitors to Hawaii. They migrate from their feeding zones in Alaska and use the islands as a nursery for their young who are born here. Females reach 45ft (14m) and the calves are 3000lbs (1360kgs) at birth and have a very close bond with their mothers who will nurse them for almost a year. They begin to show up in Maui waters in December, but there aren't many until well into January. By February and March, however, they are thick in number. The latest counts estimate the north Pacific population to be somewhere between 12,000 and 15,000 individuals with well over half this number coming to visit Hawaii at some point each winter. At times you cannot gaze at the ocean for five minutes and not see the telltale blow of these visitors. They are found throughout Hawaii at this time, but nowhere are their numbers as dense as Maui County. During this time their haunting sounds which travel for miles underwater are with you on every dive. If they are close you can even feel the vibration of these songs within the body.

The whales are Federally protected and vessels have an approach limit. This often leads to a zig-zagging route to get to some of the dive sites. At times the whales will approach a boat and the captain will have to sit in neutral until they decide to move on. This is known as a "mugging" and can last for a few minutes to hours in some cases. The other reason the whales gather in these numbers is to mate. This practice can lead to incredible surface activities as groups of males chase after a single female in hopes of fathering her next offspring. This is similar to a tourist activity that takes place most evenings throughout the various bars on Front Street in Lahaina.

Humpback "family" off Kona

Red Hill cave and monk seal

25) Puuolai (Red Hill)
Location: Makena
Depth: 20-50ft (6-16m)

Red Hill is a site that often has a mild prevailing current creating a drift dive that all levels of divers can normally handle. The site gets its name from the imposing red volcanic vent that towers above. It is a good kayak dive done off Oneuli Beach (which is a bit of a secret spot to find) but a bit far as a shore dive.

Several large boulders are areas for sleeping turtles and frogfish. Slightly deeper you will find a large expanse of calcareous algae with tiny little "satellites"

Author David Fleetham heading out for a kayak dive

of coral. Look for both species of lionfish here along with leaf scorpionfish. Back to the reef in the 20-30ft (6-9m) range are some canyons of sand between lava ridges. If there is current, this is where you will feel it the most.

As you round the corner kick into the shallows and look for a cave entrance which is more of a huge archway with a second exit. More often than not a whitetip reef shark or two will be resting back in the dark on the sandy bottom. Look above for a slit filled with soldierfish, goatfish and several species of lobster. A monk seal has even frequented this area on several occasions.

Both wide angle and macro lenses work for this dive. Back out on the reef there are many kinds of moray eels, along with octopus, flounder, goatfish, trumpetfish, bigeye soldierfish, flatworms and nudibranchs. After a three- minute stop you will surface off Little Beach, a "clothing optional" stretch of sand. Now, ahem, turn around and look for your dive boat to pick you up.

Blackside hawkfish in the coral

Green sea turtle
catching a breath

Whitetip reef shark

26) Five Graves
Location: Makena Landing
Depth: 0-35ft (0-10m)

Locally also referred to as Five Caves, this is considered a fun site that can be done from shore or by boat and obviously there are a number of caves here for divers to explore. The dive is fairly shallow and five state moorings for commercial vessels are spread evenly about, so expect to be joined by boatloads of snorkelers in the morning hours. Visibility here is usually good but can turn pretty murky sometimes.

Normally, it is easy to see and navigate the site, which consists of two main lava ridges that turn to scattered boulders as you get deeper. The wide valley between the two holds the preferred architecture for octopus to hide. Several of the caves are really a series of arches with multiple exits but some do come to a dead end and a light is recommended. Green sea turtles are prolific here along with moray eels

and schooling young unicornfish. Smaller manta rays and eagle rays cruise by fairly regularly. A large school of Hellers barracuda will sometimes drift in from the reef area that is just to the north. Inshore, a low flattened cave entrance leads to "The Bubble Cave" where you can surface into a small interior enclosure.

If there is a south swell pumping, the compression in the air space can be hard on one's ears and should be avoided. If you do this as a shore dive from Makena Landing, parking is limited. So, it is best to go early on a weekday. Restrooms and showers are an attractive sight at the end of your dive.

Hawaiian fantail filefish

27) Olowalu
Location: 6mi S of Lahaina, MM14
Depth: 0-80ft (0-25m)

Hawaiian domino damselfish

Another afternoon spot for diving or snorkeling is Olowalu, located six miles south of Lahaina. This 1,000- acre reef is the largest off Maui and holds coral colonies that are more than 300 years old. Both shore divers and charter boats frequent the area, which has been hit hard over the years by both man-made and natural occurrences.

Coral bleaching hit the entire state in 2014 and 2015, killing 20 to 40 percent of Maui's polyps. In 2017 oceanographer and Mission Blue founder Sylvia Earle named Olowalu a "Hope Spot," the first location in Hawaii to receive this designation. It was selected due to the magnitude of the reef itself and the critical role it plays in fostering huge juvenile populations. A south swell, a common occurrence in the summer months, can drop visibility to a few feet.

When visibility is clear, however, Olowalu is an impressive site with acres of finger coral dropping well offshore to the sand bottom at 80+ ft (25+m). It is over a half-mile (.8km) offshore to the turtle cleaning station area with state moorings so consider getting on a boat for this. Plan "B" is a kayak. Companies run tours here daily because of the normally calm conditions most days. More than 400 individual manta rays have been identified in the waters here.

Cruising manta

Wire coral goby

The Atlantis submarine passes by the wreck

28) The Carthaginian
Location: 1.5mi (2.4km) south of Lahaina Harbor offshore from Puamana Beach Park
Depth: 0-110ft (0-36m)

There's a lot of history in this small package beneath the sea that divers will discover when visiting and checking the past about the Carthaginian II. Lahaina was once a bustling 19th-century whaling port. How it got here is a fascinating tale. The Carthagian (I) was built in Denmark in 1921 as a majestic three- masted schooner. It was a working vessel for over 30 years working in the Baltic Sea and later in Central America, eventually landing with a new owner in San Diego.

In 1965, it was given a complete overhaul by Hollywood to be part of the movie Hawaii created after the famous Robert Michener book. The Lahaina Restoration Foundation later bought it and it served as a

Schooling goatfish at the ship's aft

112

Descending to the ship's aft

historic floating museum at the Lahaina Harbor for over 20 years. BUT, According to the United States National Register of Historic Places, Carthaginian foundered on its way to Honolulu on Easter, April 22, 1973. The ship was destroyed but the foundation was quick to find a replacement and purchased a 93ft (27.5m) German-made schooner called Komet.

After being sailed from Denmark to Maui by an all-Lahaina crew, it was transformed into a two-masted brig and rechristened Carthaginian II which became a floating whaling museum for the next 32 years. Deterioration over time closed the museum and Atlantis Submarine purchased it for an artificial reef. It was sunk in 2005 and is visited several times daily by a submarine loaded with tourists. Be aware that the current runs strong here at times. Plan accordingly. Whitetip reef sharks can often be found in the main hold and a large school of goatfish hang back at the stern. Frogfish come and go so be on the lookout for them!

At left, the Carthaginian in it's heyday

29) Mala Wharf
Location: Road off Front Street, Lahaina.
Depth: 20-40ft (6-12m)

Whitetip reef shark

You want to do this dive during the day to get a feel for the site before doing a night dive here, but you definitely should do a night dive here. Dive boats often do a second or third tank in this location because it is the perfect depth for a long bottom time and a great site for marine life. If you are shore diving enter on the south side of the wharf. It is a bit rocky getting in so be sure to wear booties with a good sole.

There is a breakwall and boat ramp on the north side so be aware that vessels overhead will be a fairly constant occurrence. The pier was built in 1922 to be used by the pineapple trade ships and barges. It had a rough life in the tropics as it was partially destroyed by hurricane Iwa in 1982. Then Hurricane Iniki in 1992 took out most of the remaining structure. As a result, big cement slabs and the pier's concrete pillars litter the bottom. For divers, this is a good thing as the poor, old pier has become habitat for lots of creatures that divers like to

Twin giant frogfish
Saddleback anemonefish

114

Mala Wharf swim-through

see. The various arches, holes and overhangs caused by the crumbling of the wharf have become home to sea turtles.

Whitetip reef sharks also like the sandy bottom for resting during the day until they are ready to prowl at night. For those who like the unusual, this place seems to have become a frogfish magnet. Look at anything and everything that might be a sponge, rock or hunk of coral as it may well be a giant frogfish (*Antennarius commerson*). They seem to be very fond of this area.

The wharf has some nice coral growths that are hiding places for smaller fishes. Mala is also an excellent place for snorkeling. But whether diving or snorkeling, only go when it's calm, check the currents and stay well away from the boat channel.

Green sea turtle in a wharf hole

Red reef lobster

30) Black Rock Beach
Location: Near Ka'anapali Beach Sheraton
Depth: 20-35ft (6-10.5m)

This dive site is located near the Sheraton Hotel on Ka'anapali Beach and can be dived from the shore after a bit of a walk and swim out from the beach. But a boat dive is easiest. It is a popular spot due to the fact it has a rocky area that holds a lot of creatures and it also has a mini-wall and some current, so drift dives can be done.

The lava rocks offer a large variety of fish and they are excellent photo subjects as snorkelers like to feed the fish here so they are pretty tame and come close to the camera. Another good thing for photogs is that there are normally a lot of green sea turtles. The currents that run through here can attract more unusual creatures like slowly cruising eagle rays.

The "Black Rock" is easy to see as it rises high above the surface then extends below to hold caves and crevices. Look for sleepy turtles in here plus eels, cowries and lots of other good stuff.

A popular night dive, see Spanish dancers, nudibranchs and lobsters. This is a popular dive so try to time it early or late in the day to miss the crowds.

Green sea turtle grabs a breath

Red-spotted nudibranch

Kiara Fleetham watches the sharks at the MOC

MAUI OCEAN CENTER

The Maui Ocean Center is an aquarium and oceanography center that is perfect for a day of off-gasing before flying home or even better, on your first day to get you up to speed on Hawaiian marine life. Located in Ma'alaea the 3 acre facility is the largest tropical reef aquarium in the Western Hemisphere and a wonderful attraction for any non-divers and children in your group. It includes exhibits on coral reef habitats, sea turtles, sharks, humpback whales and the Hawaiian culture.

From tank to tank the living reef exhibit presents over 40 Hawaiian coral species taking you from the shallows on down to the deep reef environment. Since opening in 1998 the coral colonies have been raised and maintained with seawater pumped directly from Ma'alaea Bay which the aquarium overlooks. There are numerous interactive exhibits and trained ocean naturalists offer presentations throughout the day. Look for author David Fleetham's images throughout the displays.

Two exhibits give you the underwater experience while staying dry. The first is the 750,000-gallon open ocean tank with a floor to ceiling view along with a walk through tunnel to really get the reef life experience including sharks, rays and schools of fish. I've know folks who have sat for hours getting to know all the residents.

The second is Maui Ocean Center's Sphere Theater. A humpbacks of Hawaii exhibit warms you up at the entrance and then a "film", for lack of a better term, connects you with humpbacks in their world through the integration of 4k imagery, multiple laser projectors, 3D active glasses and an impressive surround sound system. If you ever wondered what it would be like to swim with whales, this is your answer. It's as if the globe you're seated in is filled with sea water and humpbacks move in and out.

General manager Tapani Vuori told us, "We are delighted to bring the first-of-its-

Sandbar shark in the MOC big tank

kind-in-Hawaii 3D sphere where our guests are immersed underwater and come eye-to-eye with these magnificent mammals. Offered year round, the exhilarating experience stirs emotions that foster a commitment to conservation and spreads awareness of the complex social lives and migrations of whales throughout Hawaii and the world." This virtual experience utilizes the most advanced systems in lenses and seaming technology. Insider tip: Get in line early and go for a seat in the center of the top two rows.

Another section explores the early Hawaiian connection with the ocean. Far ahead of their time they understood both land and sea environments in a way that ensured their people would prosper for generations to come. Lessons we can all appreciate and learn from even today. In the center of the many buildings is an open air cafe and on the ocean side you'll find a full restaurant, so expect to spend a good part of a day here.

Aerial view of the Maui Ocean Center in Ma'alaea

Beach at Lanai

MOLOKAI & LANAI

The smallest inhabited island in Hawaii, Lanai was once known as the "Pineapple Isle" because of its large pineapple production from 1922 to 1992. Oracle CEO Larry Ellison purchased 92-percent of the island in 2012. Accommodations include Hotel Lanai in Lanai City and a Four Seasons Resort near Hulopo'e Bay, a picture-perfect conservation area that a resident group of spinner dolphins visits almost daily. Most diving is done from Maui, on vessels crossing the nine mile channel.

Molokai is known as "The Friendly Island" because it is said the 'aloha spirit' flourishes here. Kalaupapa Peninsula off the north side is famous for the leper colony cared for by Father Damien, who passed away in 1889 after contracting the disease.

Today, the trail from the cliffs above to Kalaupapa is traveled on mule and by hikers. The two-mile-long (3.2km), 300ft (91m)-wide Papohaku Beach on the west shore of Molokai is the longest white sand beach in the Hawaiian Islands.

The colorful stores and friendly people are truly Hawaii at its best.

Best of Lanai
31) First Cathedral
32) Second Cathedral
33) Shark Fin Rock
34) Barge Harbor

The Best of Molokai
35) Fish Rain
36) The Pinnacle

DIS N' DAT SHOP

HAWAII
DISDAT
ALOHA STATE

Lanai's Dis N' Dat Shop

The main entrance to First
Cathedral with divers coming in

Raccoon butterflyfish

31) First Cathedral
Location: off Pu'u Pehe Rock
Depth: 18-65ft (5-19m)

The area's two most popular sites are huge caverns named cathedrals. First Cathedral, closer to Maui, breaks the surface in front of the iconic Pu'u Pehe Rock, an 80ft (24m) volcanic monolith that stands just inshore. A plateau just offshore holds two state moorings and creates a canyon between the two. The main entrance is a short swim away at 45ft (13.5m) and has plenty of room for two divers to enter side by side. The room immediately opens up, and divers can see light filtering through the far wall like a stained-glass window, and a rock just in front is reminiscent of an altar which resulted in its name.

To the left, a wide crevice with a silt bottom stretches back into the darkness and is a favorite spot for whitetip reef sharks, goatfish and soldierfish. A round exit at the back of the cavern is known as the Toilet Bowl, where a moderate swell concentrates surge to flush a departing diver out of the opening.

In a heavy swell, dive guides will have you avoid this area and exit the same way you entered. Look for juvenile rockmover wrasse over the rubble areas and frogfish on the wall of the plateau leading back to your dive boat. If you still have air left, continue past your mooring where there's an enormous arch to explore.

Cowrie

Galapagos sharks three
miles offshore of Oahu

Tiger shark

Hawaii Sharks

There are about 40 species of sharks in Hawaii, of which eight can be observed near shore, including the whitetip reef, blacktip and tiger shark. Grey reef, blacktip, sandbar, scalloped hammerhead, oceanic whitetip, silky and Galapagos tend to be seen in deeper water or well off the coastline.

Tiger sharks are the species that most often attack humans in Hawaiian waters, but that is rare and often associated with spearfishing and/or island runoff and poor visibility... just another reason not to enter the ocean where the water is brown.

The natural power and beauty of sharks attracts divers and photographers and videographers from around the world. Sharks have always played a big role in Hawaiian culture. In the past, the animal provided the people with tools and weapons. Shark teeth, for example, were used as a knife and shark skins were used for hula drums.

Hawaiian fighting implements with shark teeth © HTA / Heather Goodman

125

Oceanic whitetip bumps the photographer's dome

But sharks also played a role in Hawaiian spirituality. Some shark species were considered equal to Hawaiian Ali'i (royalty). When a family member died, it was believed that the deceased could reincarnate in the form of a shark. This shark then was the family's 'aumakua, a guardian spirit and protector. Commercially baiting sharks for encounters close to the coastline is illegal. Just over three miles off Oahu's northshore it is possible to safely snorkel with sharks in a floating cage to get close to several deep water species.

Charters are available off Kona to see open ocean cetaceans such as pilot whales. Oceanic whitetip sharks are often following these groups, like pilot whales, and will give a snorkeler an up close and very memorable encounter. Huge schools of scalloped hammerhead sharks have also been sighted out here with their fins breaking the surface for as far as the eye can see!!

Oceanic whitetip and
pilotfish in blue water

Maui Dive Shop boat on the shallow mooring at Second Cathedral

32) Second Cathedral
Location: Two miles beyond First Cathedral
Depth: 10-70ft (3-18m)

Second Cathedral does not break the surface and is further down the south shore of Lanai. One of the two moorings here is in shallow water as the site is just ten feet down. From here if you swim west, away from Maui, you will drop into the more dramatic opening framed by volcanic archways. Look for sergeant majors tending eggs here. The cavern resembles a huge volcanic bubble that began to burst and then solidified. The main room has many entrances and exits. While a dive light is not

Sean Fleetham and schooling bluestripe snapper off Second Cathedral

A day octopus making
its way along the reef

mandatory, it is highly recommended to illuminate all the critters that hide in the corners. Among the many crustaceans that make their home here are eight different species of lobster and a variety of shrimp and crabs. Jacks will move in and out of the light and darkness looking to sneak up on a meal. Trumpetfish like the long crevices for stealth to surprise prey.

Outside the cavern are large, flittering schools of pyramid butterflyfish and an enormous school of bluestriped snapper patrols a small pinnacle on the east inshore side of the reef, which ends in a broad, sandy bottom. On the seaward side, the reef has areas of broken coral that form

patches of rubble, which is a favorite habitat for day octopi. This area is actually rather famous for its abundance of these intelligent cephalopods.

Divers who regularly glance into the blue water column can encounter an array of pelagic creatures. The whole area is fun to explore and people spend a lot of time in the chambers with dive lights poking around in the deeper reaches.

Volcanic archway of
Second Cathedral

The "Shark Fin" can be seen in the distance

33) Shark Fin Rock
Location: Kaunolu Bay
Depth: 20-80 ft (6-23m)

You are entering a very royal spot when you come into this bay. The summer home of King Kamehameha was situated on the coast here from 1790-1810. Kamehemeha would frequent Kaunolu as one of his favorite fishing grounds. Shark Fin gets its name from the shape of a lava rock that is part of a wall that breaks the surface, resembling the giant fin and back of a prehistoric shark. The state mooring for this site is just west and inshore from the rock in 60ft (18m). You will cross a sloping bottom with sparse coral growth and varying sized boulders, a perfect background for camouflaged devil scorpionfish.

On your way to the wall, if you venture towards the 80ft (24m) depth, you'll find a male bicolor anthias attempting to herd a group of females. If this is your second dive of the day, skip this and keep it above 60ft (18m). There are a couple of archways along the wall. The second one, directly below the "shark fin", is shaded and holds a colony of orange cup corals. This is a good area to find nudibranchs as well. The wall ends just past this and slopes rapidly downward. If there is current it is here that you will feel it.

Turn the corner and you will be in a valley created by a second pinnacle that does not break the surface. A vertical crevice on your left is decorated with regal slipper lobsters (*Arctides regalis*), also called shovel-nosed lobsters. The short valley opens up to a shallow reef area. Keep edging your way to your left to get back to the mooring.

Colony of beautiful cup corals

Look in the crevice for regal slipper lobsters

Tetrapod area is full of critters

34) Barge Harbor (Kaumalapau Harbor)
Location: SW Lanai
Depth: 10-110ft (3-31m)

Kaumalapau Harbor is where barges filled with pineapple would depart after dropping off goods for the residents. It is still where the majority of items come into the island. North of the channel markers for the harbor is a submerged point that drops precipitously to a pile of boulders and then turns to sand at 130ft (40m). The wall begins around 20ft (6m) so you can pick your depth to fit your desired dive time. The wall has a few "S" turns and small caves to explore until finally making the turn into the harbor

breakwall. One small cave holds rare long-handed lobster, this is the shallowest David has ever seen this species. It usually stays below safe diving levels. Look for wire corals and the accompanying wire coral goby zipping up and down its host. The corals protrude from the wall along the deeper reaches and the gobies make good macro subjects. Scalloped hammerhead sharks have been seen cruising out in the blue so glance out occasionally.

Directly inshore from the point in very shallow water is a cave/tube system dubbed "Dave's Maze", after the co-author of this book. Venture here only with a light and only if it is very calm. Any surge turns this shallow area into the diving version of a cheese grater. The walls are covered in yellow and red encrusting sponge dotted with cowry shells. Lobsters dart into deeper cavities when they detect your bubbles. Bypassing the maze, you then continue on to a slope comprised of huge concrete tetrapods that protect the harbor. This man-made tangle has created a habitat for a variety of creatures, most of whom stay back in the recesses. This has all the ingredients for a great night dive.

Longhanded lobster

Divers with wire and snowflake
coral off Kaumalapau's dropoff

Bannerfish school

35) Fish Rain
Location: E Molokai
Depth: 80-110ft (8-36m)

An overview of Maui County would be incomplete without mention of this last gem. Mokuho'oniki Rock is located in the Pailolo Channel about one mile off the east end of Molokai. The secret is to leave very early in the morning before the trade winds pick up, so go to bed early if you sign up for this one. Once you get to Mokuho'oniki there is always a place to dive and then, after your dives, the ride back to Lahaina has the trade winds behind you, so the pounding is to a minimum.

Any location around the rock is a good dive, but Fish Rain, off the corner that faces Lanai, is a favorite spot to seek sightings of scalloped hammerhead sharks. This one is for experienced divers as the site slopes down deep to 110 ft (36m). There are usually currents present as well, which is good as hammerheads like currenty areas. Toward Maui, the slope becomes a substrate of rocks and boulders that also levels out at 110 ft (36m). Look into the blue water for the hammerheads. On a good day, you may see a few or a school. If Lady Luck is with you, they will come close enough for a photo. The rare and endemic titan scorpionfish is a regular here along with huge jacks that send schools of butterflyfish, damsels and bannerfish diving for the safety of the reef.

Scalloped Hammerhead

Lahaina Divers boat off
Mokuhoʻoniki or "Elephant Rock"

Longnose hawkfish in black coral

36) The Pinnacle
Location: North side of Mokuhooniki
Depth: 35-100ft (10.5-30m)

The Pinnacle is located off the north side of Mokuhooniki and reaches to within 35 ft (10.5m) of the surface. It drops to 80 ft (24m) on the inshore side where an archway/swim-through creates a home for various species of lobster. On the Molokai side it drops past 100 ft (30m) to a thin sand bottom. There is some unexploded ordnance in this area. Divers drop into open water and quickly descend as there are no moorings on these remote sites. Some boats will anchor on the top of The Pinnacle so divers can follow the anchor line down. The current here can be quite strong and the pinnacle creates an eddy from which to hide from this. Look for colorful fish like the endemic Thompson's anthias (*Pseudanthias thompsoni*). This is special as these fish are regularly seen in the northwest atolls but are rare around the main islands. On the structure itself, there are small sprigs of black coral. Look here for longnose hawkfish. Giant frogfish frequent this sanctuary zone so check for the well-camouflaged critters. This is another area to put your head on a swivel as there are gray reef sharks, hammerheads and even whale sharks that have been sighted out into the blue water.

A male Thompson's anthias

Endemic banded spiny lobsters in
the crevices at The Pinnacle

The BIG ISLAND

Honokohau Harbor

Confusingly, Hawaii Island has the same name as the state, so, instead, locals often call it "The Big Island". It is less than one million years old and it is indeed big. At over 4000 square miles, it is more than twice the size of all the other islands combined. Kilauea Volcano off the southeast end of the island has been spewing lava down its slopes and into the Pacific since 1983, a phenomenon that just stopped as we were preparing this book in March of 2020. But it could start again any time. This is one of the most spectacular sights on the planet. Be sure and save a day or two to explore Hawaii Volcanoes National Park.

The majority of dive operators on the Big Island are found on the west side of the island on the Kona Coast. They offer daily tours to the popular spots and many do afternoon, evening and the famous manta or blackwater dives as well. At night, Kona is a bustling hive of bars and eateries.

Four volcanoes, including the world's largest, the 13,679 foot Mauna Loa, provide a unique situation here in the Pacific. First you do not have to go far offshore before you are in extremely deep water. The unique underwater topography makes it ideal to observe marine mammals and a lot of sites are accessible as the island blocks the trade winds to create fairly flat conditions. A wide variety of marine mammals that are normally only found in open ocean can be seen close in to the Big Island, including sperm whales, beaked whales, melon headed whales, pygmy

Spinners dolphins off
southern Kona coast

killer whales, false killer whales, pilot whales, rough toothed dolphin and huge groups of Pacific spotted dolphin. Now the caveat here is that this is one big ocean and I have spent many days, miles offshore and seen nothing. Some of the operators will cruise offshore in between dives but you will probably have to charter your own boat to spend an entire day miles out to sea.

There is a multitude of dive sites up and down the Kona coast and the operator you select will give you a "best bet" depending on the conditions that day.

The Big Island's surface volcanic terrain continues under the sea where molten lava cooled in steamy torrents in

Lava flowing from Kilauea reaches the Pacific Ocean off Volcanoes National Park.

Beach time at Kamakahonu Beach

the tropical sea water. This has created a diver's wonderland. Lava tubes, huge coral heads, arches and vast craters like "Au Au Crater," create a spectacular backdrop for underwater photography.

These waters hold many indigenous fish and a good part of the challenge and fun in Kona diving is to identify and digitally capture these critters. Butterflyfish, wrasses and cleaner wrasses all fall into the unique to Hawaii category. Photographers also seek less mobile subjects like Spanish dancers, turtles getting cleaned by yellow tangs, resting turtles, leaf fish and frogfish.

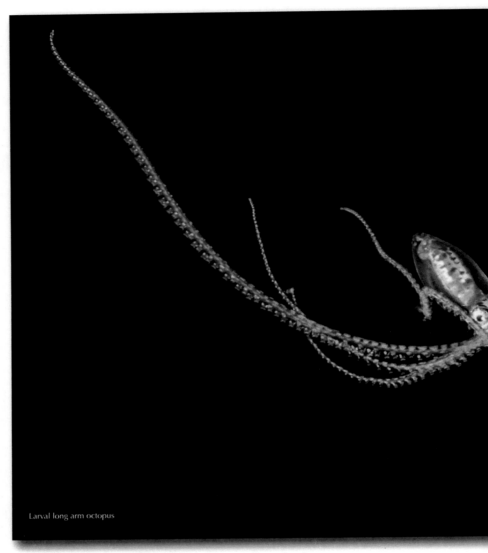

Larval long arm octopus

Blackwater Diving

For advanced divers there are blackwater night dives or "Pelagic Magic". How it works is, you go a mile or two straight out into open ocean and put down a pattern of lights and/or lines to attract marine life. Once it gets dark you slip into the nearly bottomless water, drop down 40 or 50ft (12-15m) and drift along under the boat. It is especially popular and productive off Kona. The upwellings off this coastline bring up no end of strange translucent creatures and others join them in a daily vertical migration from the dark

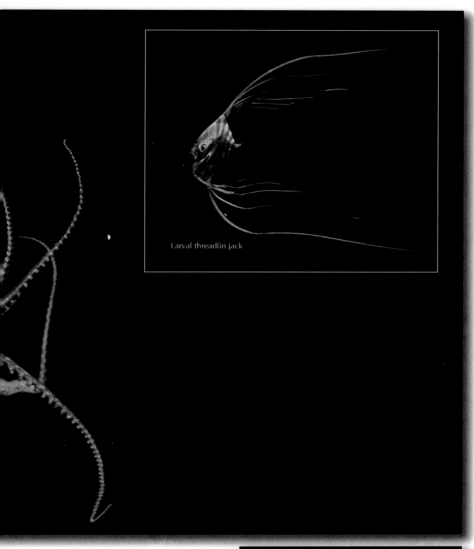

Larval threadfin jack

depths, including wild things like this neon pelagic octopus seen above. This is a situation where you need to be very comfortable with your buoyancy as there are few reference points.

This diving is becoming popular in many places in the Pacific. Hawaii is considered its birthplace. Even marlins and whale sharks show up.

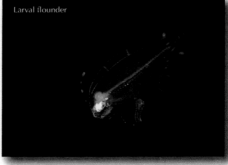

Larval flounder

Humpback pair spouting

Kona

Volcanic Hawaii, with snow at the top of its highest peaks and humpback whales frolicking in its deep blue bays, is the largest and most volcanically active island in the state. Above the surface, the lava fields of this relatively young island can be seen easily from offshore. Rivers of molten lava have hardened into expansive black fields that run down the island's many slopes and into the clear, blue sea.

The Big Island's surface volcanic terrain continues down below creating a crazy wonderland of lava arches and caves that divers love and fish find as perfect habitat. Kona is the home of many scuba operations and boat dives are the norm although there are beach dives along the coast as well.

There are also dolphin snorkeling operations on Kona that can be fun and produce nice interactions with spinners and other dolphins. The undersea topography of Kona has a series of deep shelves that attract various whales and

Bar on Alli Drive, Kona

dolphins as well as rays and whale sharks. Fast boasts, like the one Wild Hawaii uses, are ideal for observing marine mammals far out to sea and getting to their habitat quickly. The Big Island is one of the best blue water venues in the world.

At night, Kona is fun. It is full of eateries and rockin' bars. The climate is normally very pleasant and constant. Shopping provides the finest in souvenirs from T-shirts to high-end art. Overall, the whole spectrum, from whales to mantas to eels and frogfish, can be found here in the volcanic land of Aloha.

Best Dives on The Big Island

37) **Ulua Cave**
38) **Puako 76**
39) **Touch of Gray**
40) **Garden Eel Cove / Makako Bay**
41) **Pyramid Pinnacles**
42) **Suck em Up / Skull Cave**
43) **Honokahau**
44) **Kaiwi Point Blue Water**
45) **Amphitheater**
46) **The Lava Dome**
47) **Kealakekau Bay**
48) **Au Au Crater**
49) **Manuka Bay**
50) **South Point / Ka Lae Point**

Maui-based artist
Robert Lyn Nelson

Art in the Islands

The art scene in the islands is very active with artists capturing the amazing sights of Hawaii through paintings, photography, mixed media, sculpture, books and lots more. A great deal of the marine artists who sell their wares in the state either live there year 'round or have homes and are regular visitors. The award winning work of Robert Lyn Nelson on Maui at Lahaina Gallery as well as many more around the USA. Nelson is widely recognized as one of the most inspiring artists of his generation. Co-author David Fleetham, Marty Wolff and Douglas Hoffman have their beautiful photo prints for sale also on Maui. Joshua Lambus displays eerie blackwater photo work in Kona as does Kona resident marine sculptor Scott Hanson.

The wonderful thing is that the great majority of these artists are divers and freedivers, so they are sharing their firsthand experiences with ocean life in their art, as seen in the iconic image of Hanson here on page 147.

There are also fairs and festivals that provide some real bargain local works with tables of clever and creative island art.

Scott Hanson

Artist Scott Hanson and an amazing interaction
with a curious humpback whale.
Photo courtesy Masa Usioda, Blue Planet Archive

The white ulua, Caranx ignobilis, is also known as a giant trevally or jack

37) Ulua Cave
Location: North of Kawaihae Harbor
Depth: 25-90ft (7-27m)

This site is around three miles (4.8km) north of Kawaihae Harbor just beyond Kohala Ranch. A state mooring can be found not far offshore. Follow the mooring line down and you will be right on the large cavern. Over the years the original school of ulua (jacks) that frequented the cave have been hunted down to just a few who occasionally frequent the structure. A recent ban on fishing with scuba along the Kona Coast may help them boost their numbers a bit.

But, not to worry. Bring a light to illuminate the various species of lobster and shrimp found inside. A night dive here almost guarantees a crimson Spanish dancer nudibranch.

Many ledges, small caves and a boulder field surround this

Mu or bigeye emperor

Diver swims through lava cave

area. Endemic bandit angelfish are here. Adults, at seven inches, are the largest representative of this family in Hawaii. If you work your way West, the site turns to a sandy bottom and drops dramatically. This is where you can spot large pelagics including manta rays and even humpback whales have been spotted here. On your way back look for the ever vigilant mu (bigeye emperor) up in the water column and other water column fish.

The Puako dive site offers two different options (Apple Maps)

Puako

38) Puako
Location: South Kohala
Depth: 30-100ft (9-30m)

Puako is around 5mi (6.6k) south when you depart from Kawaihae Harbor and less than a mile (1k) if you put in at the Puako Boat Ramp. This area can be done as two separate dives with the north side ranging in depth from 30 to 100ft (9-30m). Eagle rays and turtles are often spotted cruising by and there is a community of endemic garden eels out in the sandy section. To the south caves and archways can be found up in the shallows where the turtles sometimes nap. Look for dolphins too.

Dropoffs can be found out in the 40 to 80ft (12-27m) zone where large moray eels occupy the cracks and crevices. Sections of rubble are a good place to look for octopus and every now and again glance up into the water column for schooling Hellers barracuda. Be prepared for current here and plan accordingly, it can be strong at times.

Endemic garden eels are found in the sand

Spinner dolphins

Divers and gray reef shark

39) A Touch of Gray
Location: NW Kona Coast
Depth: 30-90ft (9-27m)

When the dive boat stops and they say "we're here", everyone looks around and says "really?". This site sits off the coastline in what appears to be open ocean. It is actually on an enormous section of lava that continues far offshore where it is referred to as "The Grounds" by fisherman who frequent the area. The other frequent guest to this area are the humpback whales that visit Hawaii from December to April. Visibility here is often spectacular and initially when you hit the bottom it looks like a long flat expanse. It isn't unusual to drop down on a passing manta ray. A short swim from the mooring past a school of blue stripe snappers reveals a narrow canyon that runs offshore. Juvenile gray reef sharks congregate here making it much like a nursery.

The width of the canyon varies as you head offshore with it ending in an archway leading to deeper water. In shaded areas where the wall is cut back, you will find shoulderbar soldierfish. If you move slowly the sharks will stay. If you chase them with a camera they will leave, but be patient and calm. They will return. Staying still will give you the best shot at an image. Other fish schools and smaller critters are also here.

Cruising manta ray

Yellowfin goatfish school

The Sea Turtles

Numerous sea turtles take in the warm sun at Hookipa Beach on the Big Island

One marine reptile that is just about everywhere that divers dive in Hawaii is the sea turtle. Called *honu* in Hawaiian, they have played important roles in the environment of the islands and the culture of Hawaii's people. There are three species of sea turtles native to the Hawaiian Islands: the green sea, the hawksbill and the leatherback. By far, the most common is the green sea turtle, *Chelonia mydas*. When we refer to sighting them on specific dives in this book, this is the one we mean.

The majority of the population are found hundreds of miles to the north around French Frigate Shoals. Here females come to nest. They will lay over 100 eggs per nest which they bury in the sand and repeat this three to five times each season. If one of these babies survives the trek across the sand to the ocean it will then face a maze of hazards for the next five years before returning to the islands were it will begin the next stage of life. Sea birds feed on the hatchlings along with a variety of open ocean fish. A single male mahimahi was caught with 25 baby turtles in its belly.

The turtles you find around the main islands all make this journey to these shoals to mate and lay their eggs in the sand. There are some exceptions. More individuals are now being found nesting around the main

Green sea turtle

154

Rare monk seal and sea turtle
warm up in the beach sand

A green sea turtle at the MOC in Maui

islands where they were once nearly wiped out by man for their green meat, which is where the name of the green sea turtle comes from.

They were officially granted protection in 1978 and now new generations have never been hunted. This has turned Hawaii into one of the best places in the world to photograph these fascinating creatures. It is worthing noting that harassing sea turtles in any way is illegal in the state of Hawaii. Violators can be fined up to $100,000 per violation and receive jail time for interference with the turtle population.

Their other predator, the tiger shark, still exists so the turtles do not appreciate being approached when surfacing for a breath or being chased from behind by divers or

snorkelers. When you find a turtle, it will be resting on the bottom feeding on algae or being cleaned by tangs. At a cleaning station you can sometimes find over 20 individuals competing for a prime position.

The first thing to do is nothing. Stop and let them get used to your presence and the bubbles you are emitting. Slowly close the distance between the two of you, watching for them to react. They all have different personalities. Some will immediately get up and leave, and just let them, this is not the turtle you are looking for. Some will lift themselves up on their front fins. If they do this, stop moving. They will often then lower themselves back down, indicating that they are not going to swim off.

Start by coming in from the side, not head

A slow approach from the side is the best way to photograph a turtle.

on, and then, once they are comfortable, you can change your camera angle. The majority you will see will be females. You can tell as their tails are barely longer than their shells. Males tails are much larger extending beyond their rear fins.

At high tide they can often be found right up against a rocky coastline where they feed on the abundant algae that grows in the sunlit shallows. Very focused on their meal, this is when, while snorkeling, you can get some wonderful shallow images and the split half above, half below shots.

You are likely to find 100-200 green sea turtles for every hawksbill, but the hawksbills are in these waters and often stick to one territory for long periods of time. Leatherbacks are the largest of the three species of turtles found in Hawaii, reaching over 1500 lbs (680ki). Unlike the greens and hawksbills, they almost never come near the main islands. They spend all their time in open ocean feeding on jellyfish.

Tangs cleaning a green sea turtle as a paddleboarder glides by

Endemic Hawaiian garden eel

Keller Laros with a razor wrasse in the sandy flats of Garden Eel Cove

40) Garden Eel Cove / Makako Bay / Manta Ray Night Dive
Location: near Kona Airport
Depth: 20-80ft (6-24m)

This bay boasts a healthy coral reef along a shelf that starts at about 20 ft. (6m) and gently slopes to 40 ft. (12m) where the dropoff starts. The coral areas are home to a huge school of yellowstripe goatfish that make great colorful photo subjects as the school stretches far across the reef. Look also for critters that like holes that hold moray eels and barber pole cleaner shrimp. The area then slopes dramatically and stops at a black sand-covered bottom that extends as far as the eye can see. One of the big attractions is garden eels rhythmically dancing pretty much all across the plain. But the sand also holds lots of other interesting creatures like nudibranchs and the elusive razorfish wrasse. Found in wide stretches of sand like the one here, these fish will quickly disappear into the sand if they sense danger. The juvenile razorfish are especially photogenic with a long banner-like fin that comes up near the top of their heads. This shortens as they gain maturity.

Since there are a few cleaning stations here, occasionally a manta rays may come in for a quick once over from a cleaner wrasse. Spinner dolphins also may make an appearance to the glee of divers. This is the site of the famous night manta dive, as the sun goes down, divers gather overhead in boats. Manta rays come to feed off the plankton attracted by the underwater lights set up to bring in mantas for divers and snorkelers to amaze with their antics.

Manta rays swim through the plankton in a nighttime feeding frenzy

Manta Ray Night Dive

An exceptional and well-documented population of manta rays have become accustomed to several dive and snorkel boats convening on the same location each night to put down an array of lights along with dozens of self-illuminated divers.

Much local development takes place on old shoreline lavas flows and Kona is the main tourist town. One Kona hotel that was perched on the water's edge had lights shining at night into the sea. And about 25

Keller Laros briefs divers before the manta dive

years ago or so, Keller Laros, a.k.a. Manta Man, noticed the lights attracted plankton, the favorite food of manta rays. And sure enough, the mantas caught on and would feed at night, making for a truly amazing night dive.

Today, the experience has progressed into something akin to an underwater rock concert. Keller is a charismatic advocate for manta protection and research. He brings divers and snorkelers to view a beautiful Hawaiian sunset.

Set in a bay away from the hotel district and closer to the airport, divers, plankton attracting lights in hand, descend into darkness. It is then the nightlife comes alive.

Huge manta rays, in numbers that range from 2 to 30, glide in from the darkness to feed on the microscopic plankton attracted to the lights. It's an undersea lightshow/rock concert as

Undulated moray eel with its fish dinner

snorkelers, holding floating rings, float above the action. Down below lights shine and strobes flash as huge rays gobble mouthfuls of plankton inches from divers. Eels use the opportunity to hunt their prey.

Currently, thousands of manta rays are being slaughtered to supply a market for dried manta gill plates in Asia. Laros has established a foundation to help protect Kona's and the world's mantas.

To see Laros' work and see how you can help mantas worldwide... visit:

Manta Pacific Research Foundation:
https://
www.mantapacific.org

The feeding mantas come close to divers

Endemic Hawaiian flagtails

41) Pyramid Pinnacle
Location: Pine Trees area
Depth: 40-120ft (12-36m)

Pyramid Pinnacle is located in an area known as Pine Trees where there are numerous dives. As with most sites here, as you head off shore the bottom drops away well past diving limits. Not far from the mooring you will swim through a school of pyramid butterflyfish, (*Hemitaurichthys polylepis*), from which this site gets its name. Beyond this is a finger of lava that contains caverns and archways. In the shaded areas you will find delicate snowflake corals, colorful encrusting sponge, slipper lobsters and banded coral shrimp.

Take a light on this dive to really see everything that is back in the cracks and crevices including several species of moray eels. Between structures are sand channels. Take a moment here to look for peacock flounders, helmet shells and small razor wrasse which will dart down into the sand when threatened. Being close to the Manta Night Dive, mantas are always possible here.

On the inshore side, endemic Hawaiian flagtails school in the surge zone. Be wary of the shallows in the summer when large swells can pound this coastline. This area is under Kona Coast fisheries management so there can be no collecting of marine life.

Pyramid butterflyfish

162

A helmet shell munches a sea urchin

Eyes of the skull at Skull Cave

42) Suck 'em Up / Skull Cave
Location: North of Puhili Point off Kohanaiki Beach
Depth: 12-80ft (4-24m)

The first lava cavern is located in relatively shallow water with an entrance that starts at about 20' deep. It's a wide arch shaped entry with views of broad sun beams that dance on the cavern floor. As you enter the cavern, take in the beauty of this natural structure and peek into the pukas (holes) along the cavern wall or scan the skylights above. At the end of the lava cavern is a small exit. Time your departure so you can get "sucked" out with the surge. The dive guide will then lead you to a second structure at the site called Skull Cave, a roomy lava cavern with ample opportunities for exploration. Take your dive light to illuminate colorful sponges lining the cavern walls or spiny lobsters hiding in tucked away crevices. Swim through one "eye socket", through the "skull" and out the other "eye socket" of this natural structure that looks like something from a Pirates of the Caribbean movie! This is a good site for whitetip reef sharks, moray eels and colorful reef fish.

Dragon moray

Secretive, cave-dwelling mole lobster

Honokahau harbor

Tiger shark swims along
Honokahau reef

43) Honokahau
Location: Honokohau Harbor
Depth: 33-69ft (10-21m)

As you exit Honokohau Harbor there is a substantial reef dropping from the hard lava coastline on the south side down to a sand channel that extends out to the buoy marking the harbor entrance. Despite the heavy boat traffic a group of spinner dolphins are often found circling over this sand channel.

Years of charter fishing boats dumping their bait and/or entrails before coming into Honokohau has attracted sandbar sharks down past the 200 ft (65m) depth. They will occasionally come to the surface to investigate a vessel. Tiger sharks are also frequently seen from this area on in along the sand channel and even inside the harbor itself. The reef that slopes down to the sand is an enormously healthy structure of various hard corals with a huge school of yellowfin goatfish that move between the three state moorings that are found along here.

Large goatfish school

The locals jokingly refer to this as "Rip Off Reef" because of the short ride from the harbor to the dive site. Don't let this put you off, it is a wonderful dive.

167

The blue waters of Blue Water!

44) Kaiwi Point Blue Water
Location: Kaiwai Point
Depth: 10-60ft (3-18m)

Only accessible by boat, the reef at Kaiwi Point is considered to be one of the better Kona Coast dives as it is full of coral structures that attract myriad fish life!

There are a couple of moorings here depending on which part of the site you are going to dive. This site has great undersea topography with features like a beautiful cavern with light shafts shooting through the roof, a dominant lava rock rising from the sea floor to the surface and a mini-wall of sorts as part of the lava fall.

The big rock is known as "Wash Rock". Farther out, there is a very pronounced drop into the blue depths. That's what makes it good for a chance to see big creatures so look for pelagics and Kona icons like mantas, reef and tiger sharks and even humpbacks.

On the beautiful coral reefs look for reef fish like triggerfish and schools of snappers and goatfish. This is an amazing dive that offers lots of variety and diversity.

Anchorage near Wash Rock

Flameback coral shrimp

45) Amphitheater
Location: Red Hill area
Depth: 10-70ft (3-21m)

Amphitheater is one of several dive sites about eight miles south of Kailua-Kona in an area known as Red Hill. As the name suggests it is a curved lava formation close to a second site called Long Lava Tube. Ridges and overhangs are favorite spots for lobster and pairs of flameback coral shrimp more often referred to as ghost shrimp by the locals. Packs of marauders, including whitemouth morays, goatfish and trumpetfish can be seen hunting over the reef areas as a group with varying responsibilities. The eel and goatfish will corner small fish, and if it manages to elude both of them it will be picked off by the trumpetfish.

Below 40ft (12m), sections of broken coral are good places to spy day octopus perched above the bottom. They will see you before you see them, so look as far in front of you as possible for the shape of a papaya retreating into its den. Look in the coral for colorful nudibranchs and flatworms, too, these like this kind of habitat. Offshore eagle rays patrol from one site to the next.

Moray, goatfish and trumpetfish on the hunt.

Moorish idol at The Lava Dome

46) The Lava Dome
Location: Red Hill area
Depth: 30-90ft (3-27m)

The Lava Dome, referred to by some as just The Dome, was a molten bubble that solidified just as it was about to burst. The resulting cracks created several ways in and out of the large room and allow enough light to come in so that even claustrophobic divers will be comfortable inside. Technically speaking you don't need a light, but you will miss many creatures without one. Areas of soft coral and sponges are good for spotting nudibranchs.

Don't be alarmed if a yellow sponge begins to move. Sponge back crab frequently take refuge here. Back in the darker recesses bright orange clawed western lobster will clamber for the nearest crevice once illuminated. Outside, hard coral is splattered on lava fingers that extend offshore. Rare, endemic and well camouflaged titan scorpionfish hide in plain sight waiting for their next meal to swim by.

Reticulated, ornate and saddleback butterflyfish are often seen patrolling their respective territories.

Sponge crab on the move

A yellow tang (right) and chevron tang hide in the healthy corals

47) Kealakekau Bay
Location: Ka'awaloa Cove
Depth: 10-120ft (3-36m)

If you like coffee then you've come to the right place. This area is famous for Kona's tasty coffee. It is also steeped in Hawaii's ancient history. For divers and snorkelers, it is even more famous for having a healthy and diverse coral reef. There are eleven Marine Life Conservation Districts (MLCDs) in Hawaii state and five of them are on the Big Island with the Kealakekua Bay MLCD being the largest.

Said to be one of the best snorkeling spots in the state of Hawaii, it is a wonderful place to see lots of fish in normally gin clear water. Look for hard corals, lava caves, crevices and ledges down to about 30ft (9m). The best may be on the side that is normally protected in Ka'awaloa Cove which is near the historical monument. It ranges from about 10-120ft (3-36m) and holds sea turtles, octopus, sea urchins, eels, and dozens of fish species including yellow tang, bullethead parrotfish, racoon butterflyfish, Moorish idols, orangespine Unicorns, the always entertaining Hawaiian spotted boxfish and more.

Please be aware that during certain times of the year, surf can be a problem snorkelers as well as divers doing shore dives.

Raccoon butterflyfish

Day octopus perches
upright on the reef

Whitetip reef shark

48) Au Au Crater
Location: North of Milolii
Depth: 30-140 ft (9-42m)

This is a submerged volcano crater and is one of the popular dives that can range from fairly shallow to pretty deep. Depths ranging from 30 to 200ft (9-60m) open up all kinds of possibilities but one of the main reasons people come here is to see the larger

pelagics to include oceanic whitetip sharks and hammerhead sharks.

It is one of the more unusual dives off the Big Island. This lava flow formed a crater right against the shore and the seaward side of it broke off and fell into the depths. Dark sand covers the bottom and a great canyon drops precipitously down past 600ft (180m) so glance out into blue water for passing pelagics. The formations are unusually smooth and lack the cracks and crevices usually associated with lava formations. Without places to hide the tropical fish found on most reefs are strangely absent here. Your guide can take you down a bit deeper to the north where there is a possibility of seeing a Tinkers butterflyfish. When first identified, they were thought to be endemic but have since been spotted in the Marshall and Cook Islands.

Tinker's butterflyfish

Playing spinner dolphins

49) Manuka Bay
Location: Off Manuka State Park
Depth: 20-60ft (6-18m)

Manuka Bay, which sits off a rocky lava flow and a nice state park area beach, is often done by liveaboard as an afternoon/evening site, in the lee of the prevailing swell. Day boats also make the run down here and those with good land vehicles can snorkel or shore dive. Here there are usually calm enjoyable conditions…. and a spinner dolphin pod. What show of aquabatics!

Spinners are known, more so than most any other dolphin, for its jumps from the sea. They leap, spin, twist, turn, and flip in mid-air. A large group of maybe 120 dolphins may be here and play until the sun goes down.

For those who don a tank, Manuka produces Kona's usual fare of critters, including large red frogfish, spotted eagle rays, Latin snapping shrimp, chevron tangs, flame angels, the rare bi-color anthias and eels including the stunning dragon moray.

The beauty of diving here is the ease of photography and reef viewing as the water is usually extremely clear. There are many lava fingers that extend out with sandy valleys in between so lots of habitat for Manuka's critters.

Look for eagle rays swimming in the bay's waters

Spinner dolphin with round wound where a cookie cutter shark has taken a plug of its flesh

50) South Point / Ka Lae Point
Location: Southernmost Hawaii
Depth: 10-130ft (3-39m)

South Point, also known as Ka Lae, South Point is the southernmost point of Hawaii (and of the United States), and it is believed that the first Polynesians to arrive in the Hawaiian Islands landed at Ka Lae between 400 and 800 A.D. Rocky cliffs, strong ocean currents, and high winds characterize

this area, now registered as a National Historic Landmark District. It is not always diveable. When it is, expect to see most anything from whales to big sharks to pelagic fish. The currents can be strong but that also brings in the kind of marine life not seen in tamer places.

Colonial *Fushsia* flatworm

Gray reef shark.

Laysan albatross at sunset at
Midway Atoll. USFWS - Pacific

Midway Atoll

Midway Atoll is part of a chain of volcanic islands, atolls and sea mounts extending from Hawaii up to the tip of the Aleutian Islands and known as the Hawaiian Emperor sea mount chain. It consists of a somewhat circular barrier reef nearly five miles (8km) in diameter in diameter and it has several sand islets. The two significant pieces of land, Sand Island and Eastern Island, provide a habitat for millions of seabirds. Midway Atoll (Pihemanu Kauihelani in Hawaiian) is a two island atoll (North Pacific Ocean at 28°12N 177°21W) with a single major pass in. Midway is roughly equidistant between North America and Asia. Midway Atoll is an unorganized, unincorporated territory of the United States. It is the only island in the Hawaiian archipelago that is not part of the state of Hawaii. Unlike the other Hawaiian islands, Midway observes Samoa Time (UTC−11:00) which is one hour behind the time in the state of Hawaii. Midway is grouped as one of the United States Minor Outlying Islands. The Midway Atoll National Wildlife Refuge includes land and water administered by the United States Fish and Wildlife Service. The refuge and most of its surrounding area are part of the larger Papahānaumokuākea Marine National Monument.

Until 1993, the atoll was the home of the Naval Air Facility Midway Island. The Battle of Midway, which was fought from June 4 until June 6, 1942, was a critical Allied victory of the Pacific campaign of World War II. The United

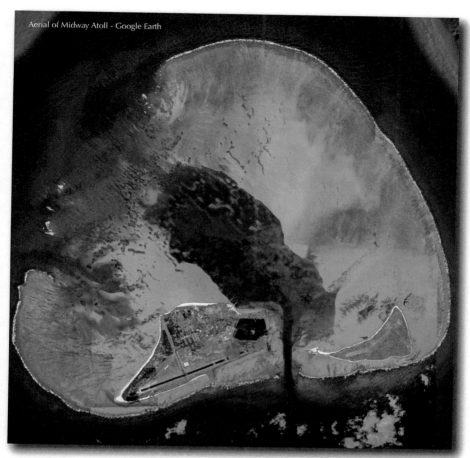
Aerial of Midway Atoll - Google Earth

States Navy successfully defended the atoll from a Japanese invasion, defeating a Japanese battle group, marking a turning point in the war in the Pacific Theater. USAAF aircraft based at the original Henderson Field on Eastern Island joined the attack against the Japanese fleet, which suffered losses of four carriers and one heavy cruiser.

Today, approximately 100 to 200 people live on the atoll, which includes staff of the U.S. Fish and Wildlife Service and contract workers. Visitation to the atoll is possible only for business reasons (which includes permanent and temporary staff, contractors and volunteers) as the tourism program has been suspended due to budget cutbacks. In 2012, the last year that the visitor program was in operation, 332 people made the trip to Midway.

Tours focused on both the unique ecology of Midway as well as its military history. The economy is derived solely from governmental sources and tourist fees. Nearly all supplies must be brought to the island by ship or plane, though a hydroponic greenhouse supplies fresh fruits and vegetables.

KAUAI, NIHAU and LEHUA ROCK

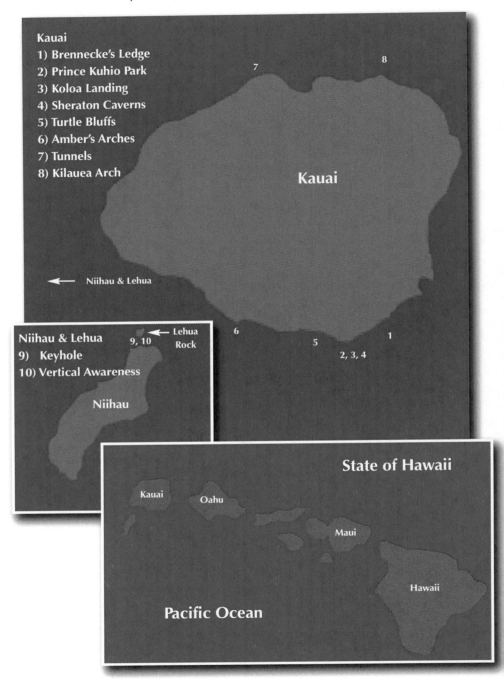

Kauai
1) Brennecke's Ledge
2) Prince Kuhio Park
3) Koloa Landing
4) Sheraton Caverns
5) Turtle Bluffs
6) Amber's Arches
7) Tunnels
8) Kilauea Arch

Kauai

← Niihau & Lehua

Niihau & Lehua
9) Keyhole
10) Vertical Awareness

9, 10

← Lehua Rock

Niihau

State of Hawaii

Kauai
Oahu
Maui
Hawaii

Pacific Ocean

The Nene (pronounced "nay-nay"), is an
endemic land bird, an endangered species and
Hawaii's state bird. Kauai's Waimea Canyon
and waterfall is the background, Hawaii.

OAHU

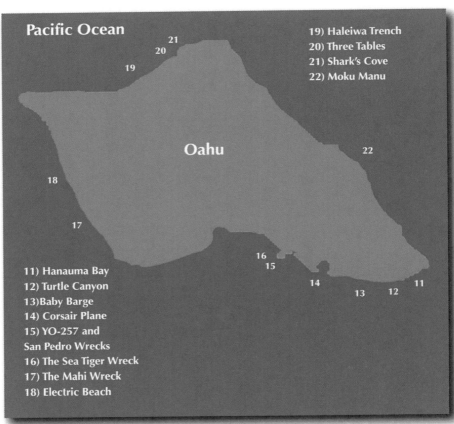

Pacific Ocean

Oahu

19) Haleiwa Trench
20) Three Tables
21) Shark's Cove
22) Moku Manu

11) Hanauma Bay
12) Turtle Canyon
13) Baby Barge
14) Corsair Plane
15) YO-257 and
San Pedro Wrecks
16) The Sea Tiger Wreck
17) The Mahi Wreck
18) Electric Beach

Humpback pectorals and rainbow ©HTA / Joe West

Heading out to surf at
Kahanamoku Beach

183

MAUI COUNTY

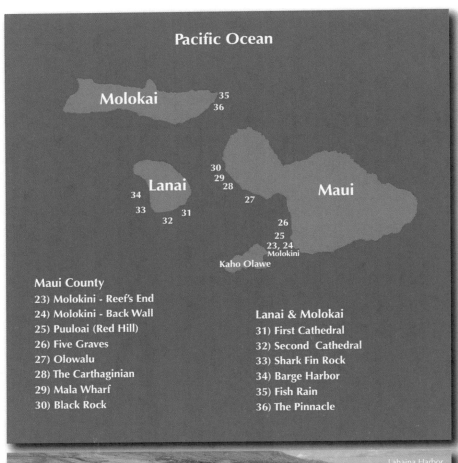

Pacific Ocean

Molokai
35
36

Lanai
30
29
28
27
34
33
32
31
26
25
23, 24
Molokini

Maui

Kaho Olawe

Maui County
23) Molokini - Reef's End
24) Molokini - Back Wall
25) Puuloai (Red Hill)
26) Five Graves
27) Olowalu
28) The Carthaginian
29) Mala Wharf
30) Black Rock

Lanai & Molokai
31) First Cathedral
32) Second Cathedral
33) Shark Fin Rock
34) Barge Harbor
35) Fish Rain
36) The Pinnacle

Lahaina Harbor

Divers on Wailea Beach

THE BIG ISLAND

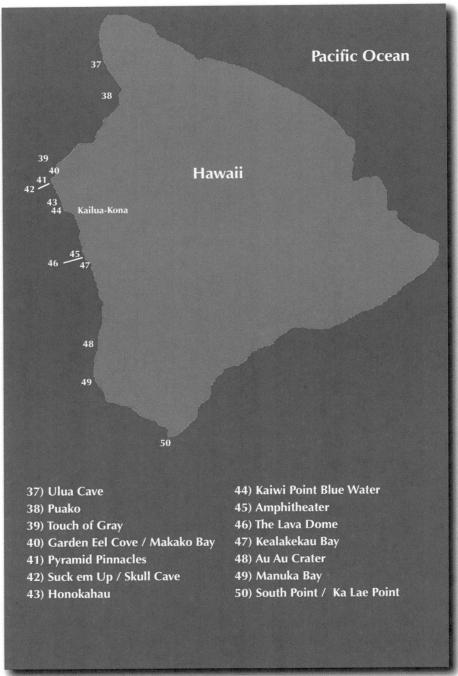

Pacific Ocean

37
38
39
40
41
42
43
44 Kailua-Kona
45
46
47
48
49
50

Hawaii

37) Ulua Cave
38) Puako
39) Touch of Gray
40) Garden Eel Cove / Makako Bay
41) Pyramid Pinnacles
42) Suck em Up / Skull Cave
43) Honokahau

44) Kaiwi Point Blue Water
45) Amphitheater
46) The Lava Dome
47) Kealakekau Bay
48) Au Au Crater
49) Manuka Bay
50) South Point / Ka Lae Point

Pahoehoe lava flowing from Kilauea that has reached the Pacific ocean near Kalapana, Big Island

Contributions and Thanks

Humpback playing

David Fleetham & Family

The authors had a wonderful time exploring the dive sites in this book and creating the vast majority of the words and images seen here. But, we were not alone in assembling the information and images for the 50 best diving sites found across this diverse state.

////

David Fleetham - Thank you to my wife Denise for all our adventures and your wisdom, support, strength and love, my best dive buddy and son Sean and my future underwater model

Kiara. You guys make it better in all ways.

////

Thanks to Neil McDaniel who was a mentor for me in the early days in Vancouver. Gary Mallender who gave me my first dive shop job, pumping tanks. To the late Jim Patterson for getting me to Maui. Pete and Jane Cambouris for putting up with me in my early days at Central Pacific Divers. To Neil Graber for turning me into captain material along with fellow dive guides Drew Bradley, Greg Wood, Paul Anka, Andy Wood, Rod and Kathy Canham, Jon Good and Al Malone. Photographer Andy Sallmon whom I have been shooting with for over 30 years. Bill Caldwell of Expeditions for getting me over to Lanai and picking me up floating around in mid channel that day. Bill and Katy Moore for a place to stay on Lanai.

Special mahalos to Mike Severns and Pauline Fiene for giving me my first captains job and showing me new ways to look at the oceans creatures. Adam Quinn for countless undersea endeavors in and out of Hawaii. The late great James Watt who is missed by so many underwater photographers. Doctor Norman Estin, of Doctors On Call Maui, my life long friend who puts me back together when I'm broken. Marty Snyderman for his friendship and camaraderie. Thanks to David Doublet for our time together in Hawaii and Mexico and for his inspirational work over the years. Jose

Luis Sanchez and Leslie Lee for so many dives along with Daves room in Topanga, and introducing me to my wife.

Numerous dive operators have gone out of their way to assist me including Marvin Otsuji of Sea Sport Divers on Kauai, Jeff Straun, Bob Chambers, Greg Shepard, captains and dive guides at Maui Dive Shop, Greg Howeth of Lahaina Divers and Jeff and Teri Leicher, Keller Laros and all the staff of Jack's Diving Locker in Kona.

////

Thanks to Russell Preston Brown of Adobe for all his assistance with Lightroom and Photoshop. The late Ike Brigham of Ikelite has helped me with my housings and strobes over the years and I'm grateful to his daughter Jean Rydberg and son John Brigham for taking up the torch (pun intended). I also would like to acknowledge Steve Kerpan of SKB Cases for keeping my cameras safe on my travels.

////

Mahalo to my good friend Robert Lyn Nelson for getting me to the Red Sea and many diving adventures around Hawaii. His award winning work is at www.robertlynnelson.com and on Maui at Lahaina Gallery as well as many more around the USA. Nelson began drawing at the age of 3 and is widely recognized as one of the most inspiring artists of his generation. He co-founded the National Marine Sanctuary Foundation with Jean-Michael Cousteau and received the NOAA Environmental Hero Award by then Vice President Al Gore for his efforts to protect the environment.

////

Tim Rock - I would like to thank many friends in Hawaii especially the late Jim "Jimbo" Watt who took a great deal of time to coach me in whale and blue water photography. Also, Scott Hanson, Doug Perrine, Masa Usioda, Stefanie Brendl, Jamie "Snapper" & Greg Kemp, Heidi "Hot Tuna" Hirsch, Kellar Laros, Amanda Steenman, James McConnell, Dan Ruth, Jeff & Teri Leicher, Aggressor Fleet and the late Jimmy Hall, Steve Drogin and Susan Dabtitz. Their friendship and spirit of sharing greatly enhanced my love for the Hawaiian Islands.

////

We were also fortunate to supplement our files with some stock imagery and additional information and photography graciously provided by the Hawaii Tourism Authority, GoHawaii, Wikipedia, Google Earth and Apple Maps.

Divers from Maui Dive Shop enter the clear water

The 50 Best Dives Books

We hope you enjoyed this book. Check out our other Top 50 Guides in this series available on Amazon, Apple and Kindle.

The 50 Best Dives in Micronesia

The 50 Best Dives in Indonesia

The 50 Best Dives in Japan

The 50 Best Dives in The Philippines

Diving & Snorkeling Guide Series
Palau-Truk-Bali-Raja Ampat & More

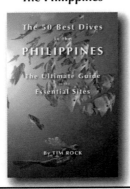

Humpback whale mother and calf
cavort along the Maui shores

A sea turtle head into the sea around
sunset time along the Kona coast

Made in the USA
Las Vegas, NV
14 December 2023

82254898R00117